Reconstructing Reason and Representation

Reconstructing Reason and Representation

Murray Clarke

A Bradford Book
The MIT Press
Cambridge, Massachusetts
London, England

This book was set in Stone Serif and Stone Sans by Graphic Composition, Inc., Athens, Georgia, and was printed and bound in the United States of America.

Library of Congress Cataloging-in-Publication Data

Clarke, Murray.
 Reconstructing reason and representation / Murray Clarke
    p. cm.
 "A Bradford book."
 Includes bibliographical references (p.   ) and index.
 ISBN 0-262-03322-4 (hc) : alk. paper
    1. Philosophy of mind. 2. Evolutionary psychology. I. Title
BD418.3.C533   2004
128'.33—dc22   2003065128

10 9 8 7 6 5 4 3 2 1

for Duchess, black labrador retriever
and possessor of all the best modules.

Contents

Preface

This book began about ten years ago when I sent a paper to Steve Stich that I had written about his book, *The Fragmentation of Reason*. In his typically generous manner, he suggested that I could strengthen my argument against him by consulting work by Leda Cosmides and John Tooby. I took him up on that suggestion. At the time, I was both shocked and intrigued by some of the central claims he had made. Much of orthodox epistemology was in jeopardy if much of what he had to say was true, and yet it was hardly obvious that he was wrong. At any rate, I published my paper as "Darwinian Algorithms and Indexical Representation" (*Philosophy of Science* 63:1, March 1996, 27–47). That paper was an ancestor of chapter 4. Subsequently, I looked more closely at the literature on evolutionary psychology and especially at the work of Leda Cosmides and John Tooby.

At a memorable conference on Philosophical Aspects of Irrationality in October of 1997 at The Université de Montréal, I presented the meliorative project with reference to evolutionary psychology to a lively group of philosophers. That paper was a cousin of chapter 5. Parts of chapter 5 are drawn from "Reliabilism and the Meliorative Project," *Proceedings of the Twentieth World Congress of Philosophy,* edited by Richard Cobb-Stevens, volume 5, 2000, 75–82 (Bowling Green, Ohio: Philosophy Documentation Center). Parts of chapter 4 are drawn from "Knowledge and Reliability," *Logic and Philosophy of Science in Quebec,* edited by R. S. Cohen and M. Marion, volume 2 in *Boston Studies in the Philosophy of Science,* 1996, 53–62 (Dordrecht: Kluner). Parts of chapter 2 are drawn from "The Mind Almost Works That Way," *Proceedings of the Hawaii International Conference on Arts and Humanities,* 2003, ISSN # 1541-5899. The rest of the book was written while I was on sabbatical during the 1999–2000 academic year at Rutgers' Philosophy Department. There I was able to try out my ideas on Steve Stich, Jerry Fodor, and Frankie Egan. Chapter 3 benefited greatly from such exchanges. At the same time, I learned what a pleasant and stimulating philosophy department Rutgers enjoys.

But there are many others who have provided useful criticism at various points on the material in this book. They include: Fred Adams, Michael Bratman, Rich Campbell, Fred Dretske, Luc Faucher, Richard Feldman, Richard Foley, Alvin Goldman, Danny Goldstick, Patricia Kitcher, Philip Kitcher, Hilary Kornblith, William Lycan, Steven Pinker, Elliot Sober, Paul Thagard, and Barry Stroud. Many thanks also to Ken Aizawa and George Pappas for providing comments on the entire manuscript. My thanks also go out to the many other people who provided salient commentary at a myriad of conferences and philosophy departments where I have read papers in recent years. I want especially to thank Leda Cosmides and John Tooby for inviting me to read a paper at the Centre for Evolutionary Psychology at the University of California, Santa Barbara, in the concluding stages of my work and for their patience with philosophical questions. Their ability to include many perspectives and approaches and still be rigorous lends credibility to the very idea of interdisciplinary work. But I owe my greatest debt to Steve Stich for inviting me to Rutgers, encouraging me at every stage, and providing detailed comments on several versions of the manuscript. His commitment to the profession is, in every sense, a model for us all. I want also to thank the Social Sciences and Humanities Research Council of Canada for their generous support and Concordia University for many research grants and for the sabbatical. My thanks to Tom Stone, Senior Editor, Judy Feldmann, and the staff at The MIT Press, for their help with this project. Thanks to the graduate students at Concordia University who read a draft of this book while attending my seminar on evolutionary psychology. Their comments were greatly appreciated.

Finally, I want to thank my spouse (and an art historian), Margaret Hodges, for allowing me the many long hours needed to think hard about philosophical issues. I would not have been able to complete this project without her understanding, love, and support. Thanks to my son, Zach, who tolerated a father preoccupied with issues unrelated to basketball. Thanks also go to my parents, William and Ethel Clarke, for their support down the decades.

1 Introduction: Massive Modularity and Coming Attractions

Not since the advent of sociobiology has an emerging, interdisciplinary sub-ject attracted as much attention as evolutionary psychology. There has been a flurry of articles and a great deal of lively debate about the status of this ex-citing new discipline.[1] Since I am a philosophical naturalist, I think it is im-portant for philosophers to learn from, and contribute to, this ongoing discussion.[2] With that in mind, my goals in this book are of two kinds. First, I want to clarify and evaluate the empirical and conceptual credentials of evolutionary psychology. Second, I want to assess the implications of evo-lutionary psychology for some issues in epistemology, philosophy of science, and philosophy of mind.

To set the stage for my project, it is first necessary to elucidate the core ideas that constitute evolutionary psychology. This is no simple task, for the following reason. Since this discipline is still in its infancy, there is no con-sensus among evolutionary psychologists as to the central topics, theories, or methods of the discipline. The best strategy to adopt, given this state of affairs, is to clarify the position of this emerging discipline's best-known advocates, Leda Cosmides and John Tooby. But their "position" is some-thing of a moving target itself in the sense that they say things that appear to be contradictory.[3] Despite this appearance, I think that they do share a coherent position. We will need to extract the essence of that position from the sometimes rhetorical prose they employ to extol their fledgling disci-pline. My strategy will be to clarify and defend this account of evolutionary psychology while, at the same time, assessing the philosophical implica-tions of it. I want to offer, in the process, a new approach to naturalized epis-temology. The idea is that we ought to allow epistemology to go modular and view knowledge as a set of natural kinds housed in a massively mod-ular mind. That is, knowledge is not a univocal concept to be clarified by a priori analysis but an empirically discovered phenomenon, like water, to be elucidated using the results of science and made consistent with other scientific results. My conviction is that if we do this, we can free epistemology from the wheel-spinning scholasticism of conceptual analysis, a strategy that, in my view, is both sterile and moribund. First, however, a brief sketch of evolutionary psychology is needed in order to provide a focus for subsequent philosophical discussion.

1.1 Transtheoretical Consistency

A fundamental methodological assumption of evolutionary psychologists is that a conceptually integrated approach to the behavioral and social sciences is needed. There must be consistency between the results of evolutionary biology, psychology, and disciplines that study culture, such as sociology and anthropology. The idea is not that the logical positivist "unity of science" hypothesis holds in the sense that there would be, in a completed science, theoretical reduction of sociology to psychology, psychology to biology, biology to chemistry, and chemistry to physics.[4] Rather, the idea is that the results of each discipline must constrain the results of the others, and so conceptual integration and multidisciplinary, multilevel compatibility is needed for transdisciplinary consistency. As Cosmides and Tooby (writing with Barkow) note: "[To] propose a psychological concept that is incompatible with evolutionary biology is as problematic as proposing a chemical reaction that violates the laws of physics" (Barkow, Cosmides, and Tooby 1992, p. 4). Once again, Cosmides and Tooby are not committed to theoretical reduction, since consistency does not imply theoretical reduction. The authors state: "The natural sciences are already mutually consistent: the laws of chemistry are compatible with the laws of physics, even though they are not reducible to them. Similarly, the theory of natural selection cannot, even in principle, be expressed solely in terms of the laws of physics and chemistry, yet it is compatible with those laws" (ibid.). Consistency, itself, is not difficult to achieve in the sense that any two true theories are consistent with each other (though truth can be difficult to determine). But, as Jerry Fodor has recently suggested, what Cosmides and Tooby really want is the stronger notion of mutual explanatory relevance (Fodor 2000, p. 82). For instance, evolutionary biology and cognitive psychology mutually constrain the range of admissible theories that the other can take in.[5]

Unlike Fodor, I do not think that Cosmides and Tooby call evolutionary psychology into being "by methodological fiat" by making this move. Instead, the idea is to employ this methodological strategy and to see what results follow from, for instance, reconfiguring what counts as an interesting experiment from the standpoint of reverse engineering. (See p. 9, this vol., for more on reverse engineering.) In the spirit of free inquiry, it is hard to imagine why we should deny Cosmides and Tooby such freedom even if we acknowledge that their approach is novel and that much of science is not so constrained. Presumably, part of the attraction and the success of their approach can be directly attributed to their willingness to do things differently. Of course, they want to encourage the scientific community to follow suit. Whether we should follow their lead is an important issue, but one that will not be directly dealt with in the following pages. At any rate, I think Fodor is right to point out that what Cosmides and Tooby call "transtheoretical consistency" is really, at the end of the day, mutual explanatory relevance among the sciences. One might think of this as a postpositivist, nonreductionist, unity of the sciences aspiration.

1.2   Universal Human Nature

Cosmides and Tooby are committed to the idea of a universal human nature at the level of evolved psychological mechanisms, or Darwinian modules, not of expressed cultural behaviors. Second, these evolved psychological mechanisms are adaptations that were constructed by natural selection over evolutionary time. Hence, Darwinian modules are innate cognitive structures whose main properties are largely determined by genetic factors. A third idea is that the evolved structure of the human mind is adapted to the way of life of Pleistocene hunter-gatherers, not necessarily to our modern circumstances. The idea is that what we think of as recent human history, that is, the last two thousand years, does not have much to do with the shaping of the human mind. This is because our minds were largely shaped by the last two million years as Pleistocene hunter-gatherers. As Cosmides and Tooby note:

Complex, functionally integrated designs like the vertebrate eye are built up slowly, change by change, subject to the constraint that each new design feature must solve a problem that affects reproduction better than the previous design. The few thousand years since the scattered appearance of agriculture is only a small stretch in evolutionary terms, less than 1% of the two million years our ancestors spent as Pleistocene hunter-gatherers. For this reason, it is unlikely that new complex designs—

ones requiring the coordinated assembly of many novel, functionally integrated features—could evolve in so few generations. (Barkow, Cosmides, and Tooby 1992, p. 5)

Even a staunch defender of the punctuated equilibrium view of evolutionary change, such as Stephen J. Gould, would not have quibbled with Cosmides and Tooby on this point.[6]

1.3   Domain Specificity

Darwinian modules are domain specific. According to Cosmides and Tooby, our minds consist mostly in "a constellation of specialized mechanisms that have domain-specific procedures, operate over domain-specific representations, or both" (Cosmides and Tooby 1994, p. 94). What this means is that a particular innate cognitive structure will respond to only a particular kind of representational input. As such, the existence of Darwinian modules seems, in principle, to limit frame and relevance problems. The "frame problem" is the question of how one can reconcile a local notion of computation with what seems to be the holism of rational inference. To wit, abductive inference seems to be able to draw on the entire corpus of one's prior epistemic commitments. As Fodor points out: "Frame problems and relevance problems are about how deeply, in the course of cognitive processing, a mind should examine its background of epistemic commitments. Modular problem solving doesn't have to worry about that sort of thing because its searches are constrained architecturally; what is in its data base can count as in the frame, and nothing else counts as relevant" (2000, pp. 63–64). The domain-specificity of Darwinian modules severely limits, ex hypothesi, frame and relevance problems.

1.4   Computational Mechanisms

Darwinian modules are also computational mechanisms. As Cosmides and Tooby put it: "our architecture resembles a confederation of hundreds or thousands of functionally dedicated computers (often called modules)" (Tooby and Cosmides 1995, p. xiii). And again: "The brain must be composed of a large collection of circuits, with different circuits specialized for solving different problems. One can think of each specialized circuit as a minicomputer that is dedicated to solving one problem. Such dedicated minicomputers are sometimes called modules" (Cosmides and Tooby 1997b, p. 81). The idea that underlies this conception is due to Turing. It was Turing who first introduced the idea that mental processes are computations. Such computational devices are classical computers. Hence, cognitive mental processes are formal operations defined on syntactically structured mental representations that are similar to sentences. A computation is a causal process that is syntactically driven. Cosmides and Tooby are not explicit about computations being classical computers, however, and so it is not clear that they take all modules to be formal operations defined on syntactically structured mental operations that are sentence-like. But, surely, many modules must be such classical computers.

1.5 Poverty of the Stimulus Arguments

Finally, some of the motivation for thinking that Darwinian modules exist comes from Chomsky's idea that poverty of the stimulus arguments determine the information a mind must have innately.[7] One must subtract the information that is in the environment from the information required for a child to attain linguistic mastery. What is left over is what the child's innate knowledge contributes to the language acquisition procedure. For evolutionary psychologists, what is left over that is innate is enormous: a mind that is largely, but not completely, constituted by hundreds or thousands of functionally dedicated computers. Darwinian modules, in sum, are innate, naturally selected, domain-specific, Turing computational mechanisms that often work alongside domain-specific bodies of data or representations. Call this the *massive modularity hypothesis*.

1.6 The Massively Modular Representation and Processor Model of Cognition (MMRP)

Cosmides and Tooby are uncommitted on the issue of connecting domain-specific computational processors with domain-specific bodies of information. As they note:

[In] reading the literature on domain-specific reasoning in children, one could come away with the impression that the study of cognition is nothing more than the study of representations. But representations are, by themselves, inert. Obviously, there must be procedures that operate on representations if the brain is to process information. So the next step for many researchers lies in discovering where the domain specificity lies—in the child's mental representations, in the procedures that operate on these representations, or in both. (Cosmides and Tooby 1994, p. 105)

Since there must be procedures that operate on representations for the brain to process information, and, indeed, if the brain were to avoid being inert, it would seem to follow that the two go together. The way that computational processors and bodies of data might go together in a massively modular mind is that both could be domain specific. As such, it might seem that it is an a priori truth that, if there are innate, domain-specific computational processors or Darwinian modules, then there must be innate, domain-specific bodies of data, or Chomsky modules, that the processors are tied to and operate on. Every domain-specific module, therefore, would be a Darwinian/Chomsky module. It follows straightaway that those, like Spelke, who argue that the infant's object concept is embodied in procedures that are domain specific but amodal in that they operate on both visual and tactile data, would be wrong to think that such data bases are domain general (Spelke 1988, 1990). At best, Spelke might say that the child's object concept is bimodal, though still domain specific. Samuels (1999) and Samuels, Stich, and Tremoulet (1998) would be, likewise, mistaken to think that one can be committed to innate, domain-specific, computational processors but not innate, domain-specific bodies of data.[8] Despite the intuition that "If there are domain-specific modules at all, then they must be Darwinian/Chomsky Modules (DCM)," Cosmides and Tooby do not take this position. That is, they think there are DCMs but that there may well be other aspects to our cognitive architecture too.

Cosmides and Tooby, in fact, do not commit themselves to the notion that the mind must be entirely modular. To a first approximation, one might think about the possibilities as being fourfold:

	Domain-specific processors (Darwinian modules)	Domain-general processors
Domain-specific bodies of data (Chomsky modules)	A	B
Domain-general bodies of data	C	D

Box A, for instance, represents the conjunction of domain-specific processors, or Darwinian modules, with domain-specific bodies of data, or Chomsky modules.

Cosmides and Tooby suggest that boxes A, B, C, and D are all live options and that these four options are not mutually exclusive (Cosmides and Tooby 1994, p. 104). Here is what they say about these four options: "Any of these possibilities may be correct. Indeed, all may be correct, although for different domains" (ibid.). Beyond proving that they do not blithely accept A as true (though they certainly think A is more likely to be true than B, C, or D), this proves that they do not think that only A need be true. They leave the door open to several of these options being true, though for different domains. For Cosmides and Tooby, the mind need not be only modular (or only massively modular). The mind, on their view, can also be nonmodular in certain respects.[9]

This claim is important since some authors, such as Fodor and Samuels, take them to task for defending the view that the mind is composed entirely of Darwinian modules.[10] In my view, the correct interpretation of Cosmides and Tooby's standpoint is that they are committed to the notion that the mind is largely composed of a vast array of Darwinian/Chomsky modules. In addition, some instances of boxes B, C, or D exist. This is fortunate, since I think that there may well be some aspects of mental architecture that are nonmodular because there is a place where, to some degree, as Fodor says, "it all comes together." If that were not possible, abductive or global inductive inference would not exist. But abductive inference, within reasonable bounds, appears to exist. It would seem to follow that the mind cannot be completely modular. (But see chapter 2 for more on this point.) We can now state the position that Cosmides and Tooby accept. The massively modular representation and processor model of cognition states that:

MMRP Principle: The mind is largely composed of a vast array of Darwinian/Chomsky modules. Caveat: There must be some box B, box C, or box D components to the mind.

Neither Cosmides and Tooby nor I are committed to the idea of an entirely modular mind. Their position, one might say, is fairly liberal concerning what might be the case. But this fact is not so much a result of a "California" attitude as it is a result of the current state of empirical play. In short, the data simply do not warrant ruling out any possibilities. At the same time, it must be emphasized that Cosmides and Tooby are certainly committed to the view that Darwinian/Chomsky modules dominate mental architecture.

1.7　Evolutionary Psychology and Human Reasoning

A significant amount of Cosmides and Tooby's work in evolutionary psychology has been devoted to the study of human reasoning. In particular, the content effects on the Wason selection task have been a benchmark for those seeking an adequate account of human reasoning in the sense that any acceptable account must explain these effects. Studies by Peter Wason (1968) and Wason and Philip Johnson-Laird (1972) demonstrated that reasoning performance on distinct tasks that require the use of a single rule of deductive inference varied as a function of the content plugged into the inference rule. This violates the most fundamental idea of formal logic, namely, that arguments are valid purely as a function of their abstract form regardless of their content. That humans consistently fail to observe the content-neutrality aspect on deductive reasoning tasks came as an enormous surprise. For instance, consider the following Wason selection task (Johnson-Laird 1983, p. 30). An experimenter lays out four cards in front of a subject with the following symbols:

E   K   4   7

The subject knows that each card has a number on one side and a letter on the other side. The experimenter now presents the following generalization to the subject:

If a card has a vowel on one side then it has an even number on the other side.

The subject's task is to turn over only those cards that need to be checked to see whether the generalization is true or false. The order of card turning is not at issue. This seemingly simple task turns out to be very hard to solve. Most everyone sees that the card with the vowel needs to be turned over. The generalization is left untouched if this card, once turned over, is even. If the card is odd, then the generalization must be false. Similarly, most subjects realize that the card bearing the consonant need not be touched since the rule says nothing about consonants. Some subjects turn the card bearing the even number; some do not. But the even card need not be turned over since whether there is a vowel or not on the other side, the conditional will be true.

The central problem concerns the card with the odd number. This card must be turned over since, if it contains a vowel, then the generalization is false. But few subjects insist on turning it over even though the reason for checking it is exactly the same as the reason for checking the card with the vowel: the generalization is clearly false where a vowel and an odd number occur on two sides of one card. Wason and Johnson-Laird tried many changes of procedure and materials in an attempt to improve performance until they found a simple alteration that had a striking effect (Johnson-Laird 1983, p. 31). When subjects were presented with four cards representing journeys, that is, with a destination on one side and a mode of transportation on the other side, the results were much better. So, with the cards

Manchester Sheffield Train Car

and the general rule

Every time I go to Manchester I travel by train

over 60 percent of subjects understood that they should turn over the card with "car" on it. This stands in sharp contrast to the previous example where almost no one understood, in the parallel case, that the odd-numbered card must be turned over. And, in the control group, just over 12 percent of the subjects made the equivalent choice where abstract materials were involved. This suggests that realistic or familiar materials produce much better results than abstract or unfamiliar materials, regardless of the fact that distinct experiments employed generalizations with the same logical form and truth conditions. Many other variations on these experiments were performed that seemed to confirm these results.

But it was Cosmides and Tooby's groundbreaking work explaining the content effects on the Wason selection task that, in part, set the stage for the more general project of evolutionary psychology. Cosmides and Tooby explained content effects by appeal to the presence or absence of a "social contract" in the selection task, rather than the Wason/Johnson-Laird associationist notion of "familiarity." Interestingly, the discussion of evolution and computation in Cosmides's award-winning 1989 article is restricted to a footnote.[11] But the idea of an innate, massively modular mind was clearly in the background. The strategy of "reverse engineering" guided the methodology of these studies. "Reverse engineering" refers to an experimental design strategy where one must attempt to determine the adaptive problems that Pleistocene hunter-gatherers faced, and then design experiments that would make perspicuous the functional adaptations that arose in response to those adaptive problems.[12] One needs to understand the design features caused by natural selection in order to clarify such complex functional adaptations. As Cosmides and Tooby note concerning the role of chance in evolution: "Random walks do not systematically build intricate and improbably functional arrangements such as the visual system, the language faculty, or motor control. The only known explanation for the existence of complex functional design in organic systems is natural selection" (Cosmides and Tooby 1994, p. 86). This point also holds true for the human reasoning capacity. As such, the reverse-engineering methodology guided Cosmides and Tooby's studies of the Wason selection task.

For philosophers, perhaps the most stunning result of empirical psychology over the past thirty years has been the deconstruction of the notion that there is an underlying Russellian psycho-logic that guides thought and language. By rigorous logical standards, humans appear to be wildly irrational in the sense that there are no truth-preserving, content-neutral, domain-general, logical systems that humans employ in everyday reasoning. We make inductive and deductive errors that are widespread and pervasive. The experimental results supporting these claims are robust and replicable. We commit the conjunction fallacy and are guilty of base-rate neglect and overconfidence.[13] In chapters 4 and 5, I review some of the empirical data concerning these studies. As earlier noted, Cosmides and Tooby have tried to overturn the interpretations of the associationism-based availability theorists, such as Wason, Kahneman and Tversky, Nisbett and Ross, and others, concerning the content effects on the Wason selection task. Associationists argue that familiarity with the data (or differential experience) explains the fact that subjects will reason in accordance with, for instance, modus tollens in some cases but violate modus tollens in other cases. The supposition by associationists was that humans do possess a domain-general, content-independent reasoning capacity. Later, pragmatic reasoning theorists, such as Cheng and Holyoak, argued for a similar domain-general reasoning capacity, but they suggested that humans employ "pragmatic reasoning schemas" that were induced through recurrent experience within goal-defined domains (Cheng and Holyoak 1985, 1989; Cheng et al. 1986). The schemas were thought to be content dependent, whereas the inductive cognitive processes that gave rise to the schemas were thought to be content independent. Differential experience explains which schemas were built and why other schemas were not built. But Cosmides tried to show that neither the associationism-based availability theory nor the induction-based pragmatic reasoning theory could explain the content effects on the Wason selection task. She argued that the presence of a social contract embedded in the Wason selection task explains the content effects. If there is a social contract involved in the task, even one that is not familiar to the subjects, then their results will be enhanced. Cosmides's prediction was confirmed by her experiments. Clearly, these empirical results challenged the truth of the availability theory.

Cheng and Holyoak argued that pragmatic reasoning schemas could explain the content effects on the Wason selection task in the sense that where a schema was ingredient, subjects would reason in accordance with the propositional calculus. Conversely, where no schema was evidenced, subjects would fail to reason in accordance with the propositional calculus. Cosmides noted that all social contract rules involve permission rules (or schemas), but not all permission rules involve a social contract. This is because the social contract statement, "If one is to take the benefit, then one must pay the cost," entails the permission rule, "If one is to take action A, then one must satisfy precondition P." But the reverse does not hold. All benefits taken are actions taken, but not all actions taken are benefits taken. As Cosmides noted: "A permission rule is also a social contract rule only when the subjects interpret the 'action to be taken' as a rationed benefit, and the 'precondition to be satisfied' as a cost requirement" (Cosmides 1989, p. 237). This makes the domain of permission schemas larger than that of social contract algorithms.

For instance, in one experiment Cosmides tested the following permission schema that was not a social contract: "If a student is to be assigned to Milton High School, then that student must live in the town of Milton." The surrounding story for this non–social contract permission problem gave the rule a social purpose: following the rule will allow the Board of Education to develop the statistics necessary to assign teachers to each school. But notice that no cost–benefit structure is built into this permission schema from the subject's standpoint. According to Cheng and Holyoak, however, permission schemas that are not social contracts should still result in content effects on Wason selection tasks, contra Cosmides's social contract theory. But this turns out not to be the case: there appear to be no content effects in such cases. Cosmides was right. Though this evidence did not constitute conclusive evidence against the pragmatic reasoning schema approach, it certainly was news.

Later, Gigerenzer and Hug (1992) duplicated Cosmides's results, but they offered a friendly amendment to those results. They agreed that the associationism-based familiarity and the pragmatic reasoning schema hypotheses were false (or likely false). But they demonstrated that, where social contracts that involved a cheater detection algorithm were involved, content effects took place. In contrast, where only a social contract was involved and there was no cheater detection algorithm, no content effects were evidenced. More recently, Cosmides and Tooby have argued that humans may be much better intuitive inductive reasoners than they are intuitive deductive reasoners. A series of studies by Cosmides and Tooby involving base-rate neglect has shown that if subjects are presented problems as involving relative frequencies, rather than single-case probabilities, the results are dramatically better. Likewise, other researchers have obtained parallel results concerning relative frequencies as applied to base-rate neglect, the conjunction fallacy, and the overconfidence bias. This evidence paints a much more positive picture of human inductive inferential capabilities than that presented by associationists and pragmatic reasoning theorists in the 1970s and 1980s, or even Cosmides and Tooby in the 1980s. However, the status of deductive reasoning remains fairly bleak by strict logical standards.

The empirical story that I have just outlined is essentially that of Cosmides and Tooby. But, as I make clear in chapter 5, there are several alternatives to their analysis of the content effects on the Wason selection task. Some of these studies are examples of evolutionary psychology, some are not. Whether or not one agrees with the methodology and results of evolutionary psychology, this much is uncontroversial: the attempt to link evolutionary theory with empirical psychology, by appeal to the methodological strategy of reverse engineering, has created a booming research industry. It is high time, then, to ask what the philosophical implications of evolutionary psychology might be.

1.8   The Philosophical Implications of MMRP

With this brief survey of Cosmides and Tooby's position concerning that part of evolutionary psychology that deals with human reasoning in hand, it is now time to map out, in rough outline, what I take to be the philosophical implications of these results. I want also to note that evolutionary psychology is a very broad research program with many topics and many viewpoints on these topics. For instance, evolutionary psychologists have written about mating strategies, mate assessment and choice, and other topics. And, Gigerenzer and Hug, Cummins, Manktelow and Over, and others have provided unique perspectives concerning, and friendly amendments to, Cosmides and Tooby's work on evolutionary psychology. In this text, I focus primarily on Cosmides and Tooby's position concerning human reasoning because that is the literature that is the most germane to the philosophical issues I want to discuss. It should also be noted that there are other accounts of modularity that differ in dramatic ways from that proposed by Cosmides and Tooby. The prime example, of course, is Jerry Fodor's account in *Modularity of Mind*. Fodor posits a nonmodular central reasoning processor, assisted by peripheral input, for example, perception, and output systems, for example, action, that are modular.

But the central rival to an account, such as Cosmides and Tooby's, that sees the mind as involving computations is connectionism. To the extent that Cosmides and Tooby see mental processes as formal operations defined on syntactically structured mental representations, their view will fly in the face of connectionism. As William Bechtel notes: "The connectionist view of computation is quite different. It focuses on causal processes by which units excite and inhibit each other and does not provide either for stored symbols or rules that govern their manipulations" (1991, p. 2). Connectionists, such as Andy Clark, deny that there is any innate representational base: "The point, however, is that the initial weights (assuming a random starting point) are not usefully seen as a set of representational elements (ask yourself what such weights represent?) and, a fortiori, the subsequent learning of the network is not usefully understood as constrained by the representational limitations of an initial 'language'" (1993, p. 36). At the same time, some connectionists do not buy into a tabula rasa model of knowledge acquisition. As Clark says: "Such a model would be implausible on well-documented empirical grounds. . . . The precise way in which knowledge about (e.g.) physics, faces, and language may be built in remains an open question, but one obvious option is for evolution to preset some or all of the weights so as to embody some initial domain knowledge" (ibid., p. 37). Subsequently, learning takes over and develops such innate knowledge. Clark suggests that individuals might acquire modular knowledge through such neural networks. On the other hand, Elman et al. do argue for a tabula rasa theory by suggesting that there are no innate representations and no innate knowledge (Elman et al. 1996, pp. 359–366). However, Elman et al. also argue that there are innate mechanisms for learning and information processing. Suffice it to say that Cosmides and Tooby's account of the mind is far from being the only game in town. That said, I will briefly summarize coming attractions.

In chapter 2, I take up foundational worries that Jerry Fodor has recently voiced against the massive modularity project. In a book entitled *The Mind Doesn't Work That Way,* Fodor argues that the "New Synthesis," that is, the evolutionary psychology of Cosmides and Tooby, Pinker, and Plotkin, is deeply flawed. Fodor thinks that what he calls the "input problem," an a priori problem, stops the New Synthesis in its tracks. He also offers several other objections to the New Synthesis. In particular, he argues that evolutionary psychology cannot accommodate global, abductive inference within the context of local, computational processors. I argue that he misinterprets the position of Cosmides and Tooby and so commits the straw man fallacy repeatedly. Moreover, I argue that the massive modularity hypothesis can be extended to explain what I call "nonexplicit, evolutionary abduction." Evaluating Fodor's critique is important because it allows us to address concerns that many cognitive scientists may have about evolutionary psychology and because it will allow a more detailed understanding of Cosmides and Tooby's understanding of their own project. In particular, and despite repeated attempts on their part to deny it (both in print and at conferences), there is a rumor going around that Cosmides and Tooby are committed to the notion of a completely modular mind. I hope to dispel this completely erroneous idea. Evolutionary psychology may ultimately provide a false picture of the mind, but a demonstration of its failings can occur only if we begin with a charitable and accurate understanding of evolutionary psychology's methodology, central claims, and the evidence for those claims.

In chapter 3, I canvas accounts of misrepresentation for a solution to the disjunction problem. The crude causal theory of representation has it that tokenings of "D" are reliably caused by D. This makes it the case that the condition governing what it means for D to be represented by "D" is identical to the condition for such a token being true. As such, it is not possible to get falsity into the picture. One might think that D-caused "D" tokenings are true and E-caused "D" tokenings are false. But this will not work. "D"s are reliably caused by the disjunctive property of being (D or E). As such, E-caused "D" tokenings are true because they are reliably caused by (D or E), and we have no theory of misrepresentation. That is the disjunction problem. I argue that it is possible to solve the disjunction problem using the resources of the massive modularity hypothesis of Cosmides and Tooby, combined with an etiological, reliable proper function account of the computational processes that constitute such modules. The result is an account of misrepresentation or error that is fully applicable to that part of the mind that is modular.

Roughly put, if the gap between the proper domain (within which the module was selected for) and the actual domain (in which we now exist) is large enough, then the proper function of a module will fail. Misrepresentation occurs when the proper domain/actual domain gap is significant and results in the malfunctioning of modules. Moreover, false types of beliefs were endemic to our forebears if they resulted in the misidentification of significant adaptive problems. Misrepresentation is part of the process that leads to the malfunctioning of modules. False beliefs about adaptive problems trigger inappropriate responses by modules. Misrepresentation triggers malfunction, and malfunction results in biological error. Conversely, true types of beliefs were important for identifying adaptive problems for our forebears. The account does not inflate the representational abilities of modules, while it succeeds in biologizing Fodor's asymmetric dependence account of misrepresentation. I dispense with the metaphysically otiose notion of a representation-consumer while preserving the core advantages of Millikan's proper function account. The account shows that meaning matters because truth and falsity matter.

In chapter 4, I argue that accurate indexical representations have been crucial for the survival and reproduction of *Homo sapiens*. Specifically, I argue that reliable processes have been selected for because of their indirect, but close, connection to true belief during the Pleistocene hunter-gatherer period of our ancestral history. True beliefs are not heritable; reliable processes are heritable. Those reliable processes connected with reasoning take the form of Darwinian algorithms: a plethora of specialized, domain-specific inference rules designed to solve specific, recurrent, adaptive problems in social exchange contexts. Humans, I argue, reason not logically, but adaptively.

In chapter 5, I first note that reliabilist and externalist conceptions of epistemic justification and knowledge face criticism from two groups: analytic epistemologists and philosophers of science. The first group criticizes naturalized epistemologists for "changing the subject" and so failing to address the long-standing issues of traditional epistemology and other important issues. The second group, ironically, criticizes naturalized epistemologists for "failing to change the subject" insofar as their work is connected to traditional, analytic epistemology, an allegedly outdated and utopian form of inquiry. Philosophers of science think that traditional epistemology is utopian because it is an attempt to respond to the unreasonably high standards that the skeptic wishes to impose on any adequate account of knowledge. According to philosophers of science, the secret is to reject those unreasonably high skeptical standards.

Clearly, both groups of critics cannot be right. I mount a case in favor of the naturalization project by first drawing a distinction between meliorative and nonmeliorative senses of justification. I use this distinction to argue that both groups of critics have missed the point of the naturalization project but for different reasons. Later, I review some of the literature on human rationality from empirical psychology and suggest how a naturalized epistemology, which takes seriously these empirical results and is informed by the meliorative–nonmeliorative distinction, might be developed. Along the way, I try to reconnect analytic epistemology with philosophy of science by showing how naturalization projects in these two areas are related. It seems to me that the time is long since due that philosophers recognize that the epistemology of the standard cognizer is continuous with the epistemology of the scientist. Quine, in my view, was right: science is just sophisticated common sense. The two roads to analytic philosophy, symbolized by Moorean informal analysis, on the one hand, and Russellian formal analysis, on the other hand, need finally to be joined once again. The way to do this, I think, is to show how a naturalized epistemology can inform, and be informed by, a naturalized philosophy of science. The two solitudes must merge.

Chapter 6 represents a departure from the previous two chapters in that its discussion centers on the massive modularity literature directly and not on rationality theory. It begins with a discussion of the objection by nonnaturalists that science has no place in matters epistemic. Nonnaturalists, such as Richard Feldman and Richard Fumerton, have argued that epistemic issues are normative or evaluative in nature. Since this is the case, it must be irrelevant to employ the factive or descriptive resources of science to reconstruct normative, epistemic notions such as justification and knowledge. I argue that nonnaturalists are simply mistaken about this since knowledge is actually a set of natural kinds that should be studied empirically, not a conceptual kind to be studied by a priori appeal to reason. I offer the "Knowledge Is a Natural Kind" argument (NKA) to support my view. In making this move, I not only depart from a central tenet of analytic epistemology, I depart from the form of analysis of justification and knowledge adopted in chapters 4 and 5. I would argue, however, that even on the terrain made possible by conceptual analysis, my views are superior to internalist conceptions of knowledge and other externalist conceptions of knowledge. But the virtue of seeing knowledge as a set of natural kinds is that the brief for a fully naturalized epistemology is now, for the first time in the history of epistemology, finally on offer. In my view, this is a novel and important methodological alteration that clears the ground for my modular account of knowledge.

In sum, my account of knowledge depends on the twin ideas that knowledge is a set of natural kinds (and not a conceptual kind) and that such knowledge is housed in a vast array of proper subsets of MMRP modules. Empirical knowledge is the result of Darwinian modules transducing sensory inputs, whereas a priori knowledge is the result of Darwinian/Chomsky modules. Such modular knowledge is instrumentally important since, once properly tethered to our desires, it results in the satisfaction of our biological needs and other goals we might have. The result is that knowledge is composed of a set of natural kinds housed in distinct modules of the mind.

1.9 Conclusion

Steve Stich argued in favor of epistemic relativism in his classic, *The Fragmentation of Reason* (1990). What I hope to show is that there is good reason to think that the more recent literature on rationality and massive modularity present us with grounds for a different picture of reason and representation. The new picture is, I believe, decidedly more optimistic than the one Stich presented. My modular conception of knowledge is a species of foundationalism, though one that conceives of knowledge not as a conceptual kind but as a set of natural kinds. As such, my account of knowledge and justification is incompatible with epistemic relativism even as it argues for the fragmentation of knowledge. Another way that I depart from Stich's relativism is that I think there are evolutionary grounds for thinking that truth did, and does, contribute to our fitness as a species. Truth and error are two sides of the representation and rationality coins that I try to reconstruct in the pages to follow, and truth connects these two key notions. In chapter 2, I look at Jerry Fodor's recent book, *The Mind Doesn't Work That Way* (2000), and his interesting criticisms of Cosmides and Tooby's New Synthesis. I will argue that Fodor simply misrepresents their position. These are the coming attractions, and now it is time for our show.

2 The Mind Almost Works That Way

In *The Mind Doesn't Work That Way*, Jerry Fodor argues that the New Synthesis, that is, the evolutionary psychology of Leda Cosmides and John Tooby, Steven Pinker, and Henry Plotkin, is irremediably flawed. Fodor thinks that what he calls the "input problem," an a priori argument, dooms the New Synthesis. He also voices several other objections to their position. Among these is the claim that evolutionary psychologists cannot explain a crucial aspect of our mental life, abductive inference. In this chapter, I argue that there are good responses to be made to all of his worries. Moreover, I offer a novel account of just how what I call "nonexplicit, evolutionary abduction" might function in the context of a massively modular mind. First, I set out Fodor's conception of evolutionary psychology.

2.1 The New Synthesis

The New Synthesis is committed, according to Fodor, to four claims. These are:

1. Turing's notion that mental processes are computations. Computational devices are classical computers. That is, cognitive mental processes, or intentional processes, are formal operations defined on syntactically structured mental representations that are similar to sentences. A computation is a causal process that is syntactically driven (Fodor 2000, pp. 3–4).

2. Chomsky's idea that poverty of the stimulus arguments determine the information a mind must have innately. That is, one must subtract the information that is in the environment from the information required for a child to attain linguistic mastery. What is left over is what the child's innate knowledge contributes to the language acquisition procedure (ibid., p. 9).

3. The mind is composed of a vast array of domain-specific, content-neutral computational processors or modules. Such modules are not systems of

representations, as with Chomskian modules, but are local processing devices that manipulate representations. Such processors may work alongside Chomskian modules. Such devices are relatively autonomous components of the mind. They receive input from, and send output to, other cognitive processes or structures, but they perform their own processes free from external systems (ibid., p. 23).

4. Human cognitive architecture is a Darwinian adaptation. These computational processors are innate cognitive structures that are wholly, or largely, determined by genetic factors. Specifically, these cognitive structures are the result of natural selection. Such modules exist because they enhanced fitness in the environment of our Pleistocene ancestors (ibid.).

2.2 Fodor's Statement of the Input Problem

What follows is a summary of Fodor's input problem. Suppose that the mind is entirely composed of two modules: M1 is for thinking about triangles (so it applies to representations of triangles but not to representations of squares), and M2 is for thinking about squares (so it applies to representations of squares but not to representations of triangles). The representational theory of mind and the computational theory of mind are in force, so that M1 and M2 respond to "formal, nonsemantic properties of their input representations" (Fodor 2000, p. 72). Call such properties P1 and P2, respectively. M1 turns on when and only when it encounters a P1 representation, and M2 turns on when and only when it encounters a P2 representation. P1 and P2 are assigned to representations before M1 and M2 are activated. A question arises here, according to Fodor: "[i]s the procedure that effects this assignment itself domain specific? That is, is there a single mechanism that takes representations at large as its input domain and assigns P1 to some of them and P2 to others? Or are there distinct mechanisms, with distinct input domains, one of which assigns P1 to its inputs and the other of which assigns P2 to its inputs?" (ibid.). More precisely:

$$\text{Option 1: All representations*} \rightarrow \text{BOX1} \rightarrow \text{P1} \vee \text{P2} \left\{ \begin{array}{l} \text{M1} \rightarrow \\ \text{M2} \rightarrow \end{array} \right.$$

$$\text{Option 2: All representations*} \left\{ \begin{array}{l} \text{BOX2} \rightarrow \text{P1} \rightarrow \text{M1} \rightarrow \\ \text{BOX3} \rightarrow \text{P2} \rightarrow \text{M2} \rightarrow \end{array} \right.$$

*That is, "all representations" other than those that are outputs of the indicated modules or boxes (Fodor 2000, p. 72).

The first option is ruled out, according to Fodor, because you are forced to postulate a mechanism, BOX1, that is less modular than M1 or M2. The mind would then fail to be massively modular in the sense that it would contain nothing but systems that are equally domain specific. Option two is no better since it faces a regress, to wit, which of the "all representations" are inputs to BOX2 and which are inputs to BOX3? Something must happen, prior to the activation of BOX2 or BOX3, that serves to formally or syntactically distinguish the representations that turn on the one as opposed to the other. As Fodor notes: "For example, the feature GOTO-BOX-2 might get attached to some representations, and the feature GOTO-BOX-3 might get attached to the rest" (2000, p. 73). But the same question arises: "Is there one domain-general system that applies to all the representations and attaches one feature to some of them and the other feature to the rest? Or are there two, modular systems, one of which attaches GOTO-BOX2 to some representations, and one of which attaches GOTO-BOX3 to the others?" (ibid.). If you choose the former mechanism then you commit yourself to a mechanism that is less modular than either BOX1 or BOX2. If you choose the latter option, you face a regress since two mechanisms are postulated that respond to a restricted input domain. The problem then is that one still needs to know how the representations in these domains were assigned the properties to which these mechanisms are selectively sensitive. In a nutshell, either one is forced to postulate a nonmodular solution to the problem or an infinite regress will follow. Neither approach will work. Hence, the massive modularity hypothesis can be shown, a priori, to be incoherent.

One way to block the regress is to postulate an empiricist picture such that sensory mechanisms or the sensorium stops the vicious regress. The sensorium is supposed to be less modular than anything else in your head. Put otherwise, nothing is in the head that was not already in the senses. As Fodor notes: "In the case sketched above, the set 'all representations' is the output of the sensorium; and, by assumption, it includes some representations that have a property that makes them GOTO-BOX1 and others have a property that makes them GOTO-BOX2" (Fodor 2000, p. 74). The problem with this view is that it is just implausible that the extensions of every category that processes in your head can distinguish correspond to something in the sensorium. Consider, for instance, the cheater detection module (CDM) that is the flagship example of a module for Cosmides and Tooby. This module is activated only when it seems as though a social exchange situation is at hand. The CDM sorts social exchange situations as either involving cheating or as not involving cheating. But this process can occur only once situations have been sorted by another mechanism, at large, as social exchange situations or as not being social exchange situations. Such a social exchange mechanism must be less domain specific than the CDM. Is this mechanism a module? If it is a module, then what about the mechanism whose outputs turn it on—to what domain is it specific? The result is a regress of modules with no end.

More important, says Fodor, is the fact that one must be able to recognize situations as involving a social exchange. But, as he notes: "So the Massive Modularity thesis can't be true unless there is, inter alia, a Module that detects the relevant Subtle Cues and infers from them that a social exchange is going on. What is the chance that a modular (viz., encapsulated, viz., computationally local) information process could draw such inferences reliably?" (Fodor 2000, pp. 76–77). According to Fodor, the chances are very slim indeed. The problem is that domain-specific, content-neutral modules do not seem capable of performing the necessary operations that would sort situations at large into social exchanges or nonsocial exchanges. As Fodor notes: "But, to repeat, figuring out whether something is a social exchange and, if it is, whether it's the kind of social exchange in which questions of cheating can arise, takes thinking" (ibid., p. 77). He continues, "Indeed, as far as anybody knows, it takes the kind of abductive reasoning that, by definition, modules don't do and that (it appears) Classical computations have no way to model" (ibid.). In other words, Fodor's claim is that not everything that is in the head is in the senses. In particular, to assume that the domains of all cognitive processors are distinguishable in the sensorium is wildly implausible, with the possible exception of perception. I think it is fair to say that Fodor thinks there has to be some place where it all comes together. That place is where abduction occurs, and abduction occurs frequently. The massive modularity thesis, ex hypothesi, cannot explain abduction; but abduction cries out for explanation, and that is why the mind cannot be totally modular.

2.3   Two Objections to Fodor's Input Problem

On Fodor's view, postulating a mind that is modular only on the periphery and nonmodular in the center solves the input problem. Abduction occurs as the result of the domain-general, content-neutral inference machine that takes inputs from the input modules and churns out beliefs that guide output, action modules. It follows that, on his view, modular, domain-specific, local computational processors simply do not have the resources to sort at-large situations. This all sounds very plausible, but is it? Consider Wason selection tasks where we use modus tollens correctly where cheater detection in social exchange contexts is involved, but violate modus tollens where it is not. On Fodor's view, we must "figure out" or "think" in such situations to determine whether we are in a social exchange context and, if we are, whether cheating is going on. Having determined that we are in a social exchange context and that cheating is occurring, we must then choose to reason in accordance with modus tollens. In other situations, after "thinking" about things, we decide that we are in a social exchange context but that cheating is not occurring, and so we choose to reason in ways that violate modus tollens. Imagine that Veronica the Veridical is at a used car lot dealing with a used car salesman, Larry the Liar. She decides that this is a social exchange context where cheating may occur. Having thought this out carefully, she decides to reason in accordance with modus tollens and proceeds to do so. We now have a nice explanation of the Wason selection task content effects—or do we?

Clearly, no one would believe this story. I doubt that we have to "figure out" or "think," *consciously or not,* through a space of cheater contexts to decide that the used car lot is in the domain of such social exchange situations. To imagine that abduction is busy micromanaging the simplest details of everyday life is just implausible. Fodor's abductive mind would quickly grind to a halt due to overload. But even if it didn't, it is wildly implausible that we would then set out to reason in a way that is in accord with modus tollens or that we have intentional control over such mechanisms. By analogy, I know that my heart must pump blood if I am to breathe and survive. But I cannot cause my heart to pump blood. Likewise, I cannot choose to reason in accord with modus tollens in one case and choose not to reason in accordance with modus tollens in another case. We may be able to monitor our reasoning performance in various situations, but it does not follow that we can exercise intentional control over such procedures very often. For this reason, Fodor is mistaken to suggest that ". . . figuring out whether something is a social exchange and, if it is, whether it's the kind of social exchange in which questions of cheating can arise, takes thinking. Indeed, as far as anybody knows, it takes the kind of abductive reasoning that, by definition, modules don't do and that (it appears) Classical computations have no way to model" (Fodor 2000, p. 77). If Veronica is Fodor's standard cognizer, then, by the time Veronica has matters sorted out, Larry has her money and she owns a wreck.

Another example will help to clarify this problem with Fodor's objections to the massive modularity hypothesis. Consider Smith. Smith is paranoid. He constantly believes that people are out to get him. His boss is trying to get him fired when he gives him more time to get a crucial report in to the bank. As he says: "He knows that if he gives me more time and I fail to write the report that I will have no excuse for my bad performance. That is why he writes 'extenuating circumstances' in my file. The boss is trying to have me fired." To us, Smith's behavior demonstrates that he has a deep paranoia that no amount of discussion will alleviate. But the problem is very real and serious for Smith. He cannot help himself. In such cases, on Fodor's account, Smith comes to a faulty abductive inference that is based on improper weighing of evidence and so forth. But notice that Smith's set of responses cannot be altered through any amount of discussion. Eventually, his psychiatrist prescribes drugs in order to control his condition. From the standpoint of the psychiatrist, the problem is that the patient has an automatic response pattern that is not cognitively penetrable. The mental states that give rise to the paranoid behavior are impervious to rational persuasion because these mental states are not under the control of the patient. What this means is that Smith lacks intentional access to the springs of his behavior in this case, and his psychiatrist cannot intervene to help Smith alter his own access to his mental states. But can we control the very inference rules that we employ under normal conditions when we are *not* considered paranoid? I do not think so. First of all, most people do not even know what modus ponens is. Second, those who know what this rule requires of us often fail to live up to its dictates in a variety of experimentally established results. Hence, the requirements of good reasoning seem to be something that is largely beyond our control. Since this is the case, Fodor has to be mistaken to argue that it is thought that occurs in contexts where we determine that a social exchange is at stake and thought that determines that a particular social exchange is also a cheater situation. More goes on than what is occurrent to thought. That is, some cognition is subdoxastic. It follows that Fodor's domain-general, content-neutral, nonmodular psycho-logic, should it exist, is severely constrained in its operations. There may well be some place where it "all comes together," but current evidence has not established this.

Fodor might well argue that some thought is subdoxastic or nonoccurrent to mind. Hence, he might concede my point that explicit thought is not likely to obtain and yet continue to argue that thought via nonconscious, abductive inference is required to sort cheater from noncheater contexts. But my objection goes deeper than his potential reply can sustain, for the following reason. If there is a cheater detection module, then thought, conscious or not, is not required, because the module is triggered automatically by the contextual cues in the environment. The very idea of "thinking about" some topic suggests intentional control of some sort. That there is some place where it "all comes together" likewise bespeaks an intentional folk psychological framework, a framework that Fodor is famous for defending. But the notion of thought, in any form, is just the wrong model for conceptualizing the cheater detection module. "Thought" plays no role in the triggering of such a device, and so Fodor's point must be rejected whichever way he construes it.

2.4 Cosmides and Tooby's "No Domain-general Architecture" Argument

Cosmides and Tooby argue that it is in principle impossible that only domain-general mechanisms have evolved. Here is how they put this point:

> [I]t is in principle impossible for a human psychology that contained nothing but domain-general mechanisms to have evolved, because such a system cannot consistently behave adaptively: It cannot solve the problems that must have been solved in ancestral environments for us to be here today. A small number of domain-general mechanisms are inadequate in principle to account for adaptive behaviour. (Cosmides and Tooby 1994, p. 90)

They offer three considerations in support of this view. These are that

1. What counts as fit behavior differs from domain to domain, so there is no domain-general criterion of success that correlates with fitness.

2. Adaptive courses of action can be neither deduced nor learned by general criteria, because they depend on statistical relationships between features of the environment, behavior, and fitness that emerge over many generations and are, therefore, not observable during a single lifetime.

3. Combinatorial explosion paralyzes any truly domain-general system when encountering real-world complexity (ibid., p. 91).

Fodor argues against all three reasons advanced by Cosmides and Tooby. I consider each of these points in turn.

2.5 Reason 1

Against the first claim, Fodor argues that there is a domain-general criterion of success that correlates with fitness, namely, truth. Cosmides and Tooby had suggested that a domain-general learning mechanism guiding an ancestral hunter-gatherer might infer, for instance, that sexual intercourse is a necessary condition for producing offspring. But this would be quickly selected out, they say, because sex with kin would be disastrous. Hence, there will be no such domain-general criteria of success because what counts as adaptive error differs from domain to domain. They go on to suggest that cognitive psychologists have ignored the regulation of action by such diverse error strategies because of a focus on knowledge acquisition. On their view, such knowledge must be coordinated with action for it to be valuable. I think Fodor just misses their point here. The point is not that truth does not matter for the massive modularity view. Truth does matter. The point is that what counts in a particular type of context as error is variable. But, of course, that fact is compatible with the fact that truth will be important regardless of the context. When Cosmides and Tooby suggest that there is no domain-general criterion of success or failure that is correlated with fitness, what they mean is that there is no particular factual matter that all situations of error have in common. Fodor distorts their claim when he points out that truth is such a fact. Clearly, they are referring to empirical properties of situations, for example, incest, not the logical properties that describe such situations, for example, truth, that Fodor has in mind. Perhaps Cosmides and Tooby were not as clear as they should have been, but I doubt it. Fodor simply distorts their view.

2.6 Reason 2

Fodor also objects to Cosmides and Tooby's second consideration in favor of the conclusion that a domain-general psychological architecture cannot guide behavior. Cosmides and Tooby argue that many relationships necessary to the successful regulation of action cannot be observed by any individual during her lifetime and so cannot be the result of a domain-general, nonmodular learning mechanism that has only perceptual information. As they note:

For example, how would a general-purpose mechanism situated in an ancestral hunter-gatherer ever discover that it should regulate behaviour in approximate accordance with Hamilton's kin selection equation—that X should help Y whenever Cx < RxyBy? When an individual sees a relative, there is nothing in the stimulus array that tells her how much she should help that relative. And there is no consequence that she can observe that tells her whether, from a fitness point of view, she helped too much, not enough, or just the right amount. (Cosmides and Tooby 1994, p. 93)

In this equation, "R" refers to relative, "C" is cost, and "B" is benefit; "X" and "Y" are two arbitrary individuals. The equation suggests that some individual, X, will help another individual, Y, just in case the cost to X is less than the benefit to Y, and as a function of the degree of genetic commonality of X and Y. The point of the example is to illustrate the idea that no domain-general, nonmodular learning mechanism, using only perceptual information, could have arrived at this fitness-enhancing equation. The reason is that a person using induction will not have available to her the intergenerational, statistical data necessary to arrive at this result. Natural selection, in contrast, will be able to respond to statistical relationships between features of the environment, behavior, and fitness that emerge over many generations. Such information is not available during an individual's lifetime.

Fodor's response to this argument is to point out that learning is often sensitive to phenotypic differences that are invisible to adaptation. Fodor's example concerns the fact that he "learned" to distinguish between Hegelian idealists and Kantian idealists, or between positivists and pragmatists, or between property dualists and substance dualists. Fodor intends these distinctions to be examples of phenotypic differences. His conclusion is that there cannot be any general argument that selection is sensitive to subtler distinctions than learning. Admittedly, adaptation is insensitive to these distinctions, so Fodor is correct to point this out. And, if Cosmides and Tooby had argued that, in general, selection is more sensitive to subtle distinctions than learning, then he would have made his point. Unfortunately, Cosmides and Tooby are not arguing that selection will always be more sensitive than learning to states of the world. Rather, the idea is that selection will be more sensitive than learning to matters concerning fitness where phenotypic properties are concerned. Where states of the world have no bearing on fitness, they clearly would not want to say that selection plays any role at all.

Consider this example. Suppose that a rudimentary causal reasoning mechanism was selected for in order that we might avoid predators. Later, that capacity is used to guide someone playing billiards. As it turns out, the table one is using is fixed such that standard causal effects do not occur. One strikes the eight ball in the way that one ordinarily would and it goes toward the right end pocket, but the white ball goes into the left side pocket, and, so, you scratch. Unknown to you, a metal core has been placed in the white ball, and so it responds to the magnet in the left side pocket. Your opponent has set you up and easily wins the game. His learning has undone your native causal reasoning mechanism. This is a case where learning has an advantage over an innate causal reasoning mechanism, but it is not an objection to Cosmides and Tooby's argument. Why? The example is not an objection to Cosmides and Tooby's position for the simple reason that there may be all sorts of "free rider" effects of a mechanism that have no bearing on fitness. The reasoning guiding moves in a billiard game may be the consequence of mechanisms that were selected for without billiard games having any bearing on an individual's fitness. The same point holds with respect to Fodor's example. Beliefs about philosophical positions are simply not phenotypic properties or traits of individuals. As such, they are irrelevant to issues concerning fitness and selection. The result is that his example does not begin to provide a counterexample to Cosmides and Tooby's argument, since fitness is not at issue in his example. In contrast, their argument is specifically restricted to contexts where fitness is at issue.

Fodor also claims that poverty of the stimulus arguments work only where innateness is at issue, not modularity. Since Cosmides and Tooby attempt to run this sort of argument concerning modularity, their result will not follow. In effect, his claim is that one can employ a domain-general, nonmodular learning mechanism alongside all sorts of innate information. One might, for instance, conjoin a domain-general reasoning device with domain-specific sets of representations or modules of knowledge (cf. Carey and Spelke 1994). Hence, it is not the case that all the domain-general learning device has access to is an immediate stimulus array of information, or even perceptual evidence from a single life (as with Cosmides and Tooby). Fodor is correct about this point. But Cosmides and Tooby would not object since they agree that some domain-general, nonmodular mechanisms may exist. As they say: "In short, although some mechanisms in the cognitive architecture may be domain-general, these could not have produced fit behaviour under Pleistocene conditions (and therefore could not have been selected for) unless they were embedded in a constellation of specialized mechanisms that have domain-specific procedures, or operate over domain-specific representations, or both" (Cosmides and Tooby 1994, p. 94). The point that Cosmides and Tooby are making is that a completely domain-general, nonmodular learning mechanism that had only perceptual input could not have evolved. They do not intend to rule out a model of cognitive architecture where a domain-general, nonmodular learning mechanism is conjoined with a set of domain-specific modules of knowledge, or what Richard Samuels has recently called the Library Model of cognition (Samuels 1998). Cosmides and Tooby are explicit about the various possibilities that are still open with respect to the domain-general/domain-specific, computational modules/representational modules debate when they say: "Any of these possibilities may be correct" (Cosmides and Tooby 1994, p. 104). What they do rule out, however, is the possibility that we might have a domain-general, nonmodular learning mechanism conjoined with only perceptual information. It is only this point that they intend to defend with their second consideration.

2.7   Reason 3

The third consideration that Cosmides and Tooby offer against the existence of a domain-general, nonmodular, evolved architecture that has access only to perceptual information is as follows. They suggest that such an architecture would be paralyzed by combinatorial explosion. The idea is that such a system would have to consider every possibility that it can define before it could arrive at a solution to an adaptive problem. But the set of such possibilities would, for any reasonably complex adaptive problem, be exponential. As they point out: "By the time you analyze any biological problem of routine complexity, a mechanism that contains no domain-specific rules of relevance, procedural knowledge, or privileged hypotheses could not solve the problem in the amount of time the organism has to solve it" (Cosmides and Tooby 1994, p. 94). Fodor makes two points in response to their argument. The first is a repetition of the point made concerning argument 2, that Cosmides and Tooby must not run poverty of the stimulus arguments concerning modularity since such arguments can only succeed concerning innate knowledge. In other words, combinatorial explosion will not occur once we grant that a domain-general, nonmodular, evolved architecture is compatible with innate, domain-specific knowledge. Fodor is correct about this point, but they are not objecting to the model he describes. Hence, Fodor just misses the point here.

Fodor also points out that Cosmides and Tooby are wrong to think that massive modularity is the only alternative to combinatorial explosion. As Fodor says: "The most they have a right to is that either we have the kind of cognitive architecture in which massive modularity avoids an explosion of Classical computation, or that (at least some) of our mental processes aren't Classical computations" (2000, pp. 70–71). Fodor urges us to take the second alternative seriously. That is, he thinks that some of our mental processes aren't classical computations. The problem with this objection should be clear by now. Namely, Cosmides and Tooby explicitly do not rule out the possibility that some of our mental processes are not classical computations. Their only point is that our mental processes cannot all be the result of a domain-general, nonmodular, evolved architecture.

2.8   Terminal Abduction

Fodor believes that Cosmides and Tooby cannot accommodate the existence of abductive inference within their theory. Since he believes that abductive inference is central to science and ordinary inferential practices, he thinks this is a major problem for their conception of evolutionary psychology. The problem is that they are committed to Turing's classical conception of computation whereby cognitive processes are causal only if they are syntactic. Recall that, for Turing, cognitive mental processes are formal operations defined on syntactically structured mental representations that are similar to sentences. This leads him to express the "causal only if syntactic" point by appealing to principle E:

Only essential properties of a mental representation can determine its causal role in a mental life. (Fodor 2000, p. 24)

Syntactic properties of mental representations are essential properties because the syntactic properties of any representation are ipso facto essential. But mental processes are sensitive to the syntax of mental representations because mental processes are computations. Hence, mental processes are ipso facto insensitive to context-dependent properties of mental representations. The problem is that there seem to be context-dependent determinants of the causal roles of mental representations in some cognitive processes, and these will be nonessential properties of mental representations. As such, these properties cannot be syntactic, and so some mental processes must not be computations.

The notion of simplicity is one example of a context-dependent property of mental representations to which cognitive processes are responsive. It seems to be part of what it is to be rational, Fodor thinks, to prefer the simpler of two competing beliefs (ceteris paribus). But the same thought that serves to complicate one theory might serve to simplify another. For instance, the thought that there will be no wind tomorrow complicates your arrangements if you intend to sail to Chicago but does not do so if you intend to fly, drive, or walk there. Despite this, the syntax of the mental representation that asserts the thought "no wind tomorrow" is the same regardless of the plan it is attached to. So the complexity of a thought depends on its context. This is what cannot be the case if the syntax of a representation is an essential property and so does not change when a representation is transported from one context to another. The simplicity of a thought does not seem to supervene on its syntax, but, according to Cosmides and Tooby, the simplicity of a thought must supervene on its syntax if the mind is composed of nothing but classical, Turing, local computations. As Fodor sums up:

Inferences in which features of an embedding theory affect the inferential-cum-causal-roles of their constituent beliefs are what philosophers sometimes call "global" or "abductive" or "holistic" or "inferences to the best explanation." From now on, I'll use these terms more or less interchangeably. What they have in common, from the point of view of E(CTM), is that they are presumptive examples where the determinants of the computational role of a mental representation can shift from context to context; hence where the computational role of a mental representation is *not* determined by its individuating properties; hence where the computational role of a mental representation is not determined by its syntax. That is: what they have in common, from the point of view of E(CTM), is that they are all presumptive counterexamples. (2000, p. 28)

Note that E(CTM) refers to the application of principle E to the computational theory of mind. Appeals to simplicity, we are to understand, constitute an example of abductive inference. Clearly, appeals to simplicity or any other such considerations that guide abductive inference constitute a problem if Cosmides and Tooby believe that all mental processes are local computations. Indeed, their appeal to transtheoretical consistency as a key to successful science would constitute an example of abductive inference and so be impossible if only local computation exists in the mind. Is there any way to save Cosmides and Tooby from terminal abduction here?

I think there is. The position that I attributed to Cosmides and Tooby in chapter 1 is that the mind consists of a vast array of Darwinian/Chomsky modules, supplemented by some box B, C, or D modules. That is, they explicitly argue that the mind does not consist entirely of Darwinian/Chomsky modules. Since this is the case, it follows that the mind does not engage only in local, Turing computations. Their position leaves open the possibility that abductive inference occurs sometimes. In particular, the existence of box D modules consisting of domain-general processors operating on domain-general bodies of data demonstrates that Fodor's representation of Cosmides and Tooby's position is simply wrong. Cosmides and Tooby explicitly argued for the existence of box D modules that are Bayesian inductive modules in a 1996 paper in *Cognition*. Of course, this is not an abduction module. Certainly, it is true that Cosmides and Tooby do not explicitly discuss abductive inference, and this does constitute a failing on their part. But it does not follow from that fact that their theory is incompatible with the existence of abductive inference. For the reasons I have just mentioned, contra Fodor, I think Cosmides and Tooby's position is compatible with the existence of abductive inference.

A distinct issue concerns the nature and prevalence of abductive inference in human inferential practices. Philosophers of science such as Richard Boyd and Bas van Fraassen have helped to clarify the role that abduction plays in science. In his book, *Thought,* Gilbert Harman originally helped to elucidate this notion. On the other hand, Quine and Kuhn have emphasized the nature of meaning holism and confirmation holism.[1] It should be noted that the latter is a species of inductive inference, not abductive inference. And meaning holism, though not confirmation holism, received rough treatment in Fodor and Le Pore's *Holism: A Shopper's Guide* (1992). In philosophy of language and epistemology, the notion of a coherence account of truth and justification has not fared well in this century either. It was Russell and Moore who were instrumental in criticizing the coherence account of truth. More recently, the coherence account of justification and knowledge advocated (but later rejected) by Laurence Bonjour has received heavy criticism from a variety of authors, such as Hilary Kornblith.[2] In short, various kinds of holistic inference have faced an uphill battle for credibility both with respect to clarification and, more important, practical applicability.

The psychological requirements of abductive inference are daunting. For instance, Miller's "magical" number seven acts as a limit on the number of propositions that one can occurrently keep in mind. And, as Christopher Cherniak has emphasized, the epistemic implications of complexity theory impose important constraints on abduction.[3] For consider a surprising result from this branch of computer science that is concerned with determining the computational feasibility of various classes of algorithm. One might like to check one's beliefs for truth-functional consistency by appeal to the truth table method. This turns out to be unfeasible for both humans and any computer that we might build. As Cherniak dramatically makes the point:

Suppose that each line of the truth table for the conjunction of all [of a person's] beliefs could be checked in the time a light ray takes to traverse the diameter of a proton, an appropriate "supercycle" time, and suppose that the computer was permitted to run for twenty billion years, the estimated time from the "big bang" dawn of the universe to the present. A belief system containing only 138 logically independent propositions would overwhelm the time resources of this supermachine. (1986, p. 93)

Given that human belief systems contain many more beliefs than 138, it follows that we can never check our belief systems for truth-functional consistency. The idea, then, of a coherence theory of justification and knowledge that requires of us that we check, not only for the truth-functional consistency of our belief system, but that there is appropriate explanatory relevance connections between our beliefs, is a nonstarter. Humans simply cannot execute the necessary inferential procedures. Explicit abductive inference writ large is not in the cards for humans. And, in fact, the reason that this is so should be clear. A massively modular mind is not the sort of mind from which we should expect such remarkable achievements.

It may be that some sort of limited abductive ability constitutes part of the mental architecture that humans employ, but clearly there are severe limits on the abilities of such a global mechanism. If the results of empirical psychology have taught us anything over the past thirty years, surely they have taught us that we must accept the fact that humans do not possess anything like the powerful, underlying psycho-logic that Bertrand Russell posited at the beginning of the twentieth century. I conclude that Cosmides and Tooby need not lose too much sleep worrying about the pervasive role of abductive inference in human mental architecture. If anything, philosophers may well be guilty of exaggerating the role of abduction in philosophy of mind and science, and in epistemology.

It might be argued that neither Fodor's conception of abduction nor Bonjour's earlier defense of the coherence account of justification and knowledge requires of us that we check for truth-functional consistency in our belief set. Let's consider Fodor. He thinks that in science we can engage in abductive inference to arrive at theories that are simpler than their rivals. Simplicity, of course, has a checkered history in philosophy of science insofar as plausible definitions of it are hard to come by. But let's assume, for present purposes, that such a definition is forthcoming. An aspect of any such definition of simplicity must be that there are no redundant theoretical sentences or at least fewer redundant sentences in our best theories than their competitors relative to the appropriate set of observation sentences (assuming, for the moment, that a theory is a set of sentences). But it is exactly here that Cherniak would suggest that we cannot execute the needed abductive inference, part of which requires that we check for truth-functional consistency in order to arrive at the simplest theory. Similar comments apply to Bonjour insofar as he requires that one be able to tell (since he is an internalist) that a theory is coherent, since part of coherence involves consistency (but also rich explanatory connections). At the base of the problem in all these cases is a holistic epistemic requirement that is humanly nonexecutable. If one requires that the cognizer be able to tell that a holistic constraint has been satisfied, then, given the results of Miller and Cherniak, such accounts must fail.

2.9   Evolutionary Abduction

That said, there may well be a kind of nonexplicit, abductive inference that figures in evolution. I want to offer a suggestion as to how—within the framework of the massive modularity hypothesis—abduction might function, specifically in the context of means–end reasoning to connect input modules and output modules. I think that natural selection is the mother of abductive inference and that it is evidenced for a variety of species in all sorts of subdoxastic means–end reasoning contexts. I will eventually discuss two representative cases to illustrate this suggestion, namely, dead reckoning and spatial reorientation. But first I consider how Fodor makes his case against evolutionary psychology in an essay from *In Critical Condition* (1998). Once again Fodor will focus on the inability of evolutionary psychologists to explain abduction.

In chapter 17 of *In Critical Condition*, Fodor criticizes books by Pinker and Plotkin that defend evolutionary psychology. He begins by noting that Turing's invention of mechanical rationality is the single most important result in cognitive science. It's a remarkable fact that one can tell just by looking at a sentence of the syntactic form "p and q" that it is true if and only if p and q are both true. One need not know what p or q means, nor anything about the nonlinguistic world. Hence, some inferences are rational just in virtue of the syntax of the sentences that enter into them or the shapes of these sentences. Turing noticed, says Fodor, that when an inference is formal as in our example, a machine can be made to execute the inference. Machines can be made to respond to syntactic relations between sentences. For instance, a machine can be made that will accept only arguments that are valid. Rational machines are possible, such as the computer.

A further extension of this idea is that what makes minds rational is their ability to perform computations on thoughts, if such thoughts are syntactically structured like sentences and computations are formal operations of the sort Turing had in mind. According to evolutionary psychologists, it is in this sense that thinking is a kind of computation. As Fodor notes: "It has proved to be a simply terrific idea. Like Truth, Beauty, and Virtue, Rationality is a normative notion; the computational theory of mind is the first time in all of intellectual history that a science has been made out of one of those. If God were to stop the show now and ask us what we've discovered about how we think, Turing's theory of computation is by far the best thing that we could offer. But" (1998, p. 205)—"But" this account of computation is local in two senses. It does not look past the form of sentences to their meanings and it assumes that the role of thoughts is determined entirely by their local, syntactic structure. But some rational processes, Fodor urges, are not local in either sense. Semantic or global features of mental processes are beyond Turing's kind of computational rationality. Fodor thinks a great deal of rational belief-formation involves inference to the best explanation. And, inference to the best explanation involves semantic or global features of mental processes. As Fodor says:

You're given what perception presents to you as currently the fact, and you're given what memory presents to you as the beliefs that you've formed til now. Your cognitive problem is to find and adopt whatever new beliefs are best confirmed on balance. "Best confirmed beliefs on balance" means something like: the strongest and simplest relevant beliefs that are consistent with as many of one's prior epistemic commitments as possible. But, as far as anybody knows, relevance, strength, simplicity, centrality, and the like are properties, not of single sentences, but of whole belief systems, and there's no reason at all to suppose that such global properties of belief systems are syntactic. (Ibid., pp. 205–206)

Fodor acknowledges that our best cognitive science is the psychology of language and of perception. In these areas, local, modular solutions have been nicely developed. The global aspect of cognition shows up most clearly, he thinks, in commonsense reasoning. Unfortunately, we lack a developed theory about such commonsense reasoning. This sort of reasoning is what computers lack and what Turing's theory cannot explain, and we have no idea what to do about the situation. In short, abductive inference or "inference to the best explanation" is global. But the massive modularity hypothesis posits only local, Turing-style computational processors. Hence, the massive modularity theorists cannot explain, inter alia, abduction. Moreover, it follows that the massive modularity hypothesis cannot be the entire story about cognition. There must be some place where things come together that is nonmodular such that commonsense reasoning can take place. No matter how massively modular the mind is, we cannot explain abduction by appeal to local computation. So says Fodor. As mentioned in 1.6, it is fortunate that no one is committed to the idea of an entirely modular mind. But Cosmides and Tooby certainly believe that Darwinian/Chomsky modules dominate mental architecture.

Suppose that Cosmides and Tooby's MMRP model of the mind, as outlined in chapter 1, is approximately correct. Suppose also that Fodor has misread Cosmides and Tooby in the ways that I have suggested. That is, suppose that Cosmides and Tooby do not rule out Box B, C, or D cases. The fact remains that Cosmides and Tooby just do not have much to say about abductive inference, or about the connection between input and output modules. Where Fodor can appeal to his nonmodular central processor that handles data from input modules and coordinates output responses through action-guiding modules by appeal to abductive inference, Cosmides and Tooby lack a detailed story about input module/output module connections. More importantly, Cosmides and Tooby need to say how abductive inference figures, if at all, in a massively modular mind. To address this issue, I turn to empirical work by Charles Gallistel, Hermer, and Spelke, that I think will be of some help.

2.10   Gallistel, Hermer, and Spelke

Rat Navigation

In this part of the chapter, I want to clarify the role that abductive inference might play within the MMRP picture of the mind. My suggestion will be that abductive inference supervenes on means–end reasoning. The result is that means–end reasoning modules have been selected for that link input modules with output modules. In *The Organization of Learning*, Charles Gallistel argued that dead reckoning occurs in the process whereby, for instance, ants and rats navigate their environment searching for food and return home, and migratory birds set out from Nova Scotia en route to Argentina. Dead reckoning refers to the process "of updating one's position on the basis of how fast one has been moving, in what direction, [and] for how long" (Gallistel 1990, p. 4). Gallistel thinks that many species possess dead reckoning submodules that together with an internal map of their environment allow piloting, for example, navigation done via a map and the observation of points on that map. In effect, many species possess something like an innate GM "on star" system. The map that rats employ depicts representations of geometrical relationships from its environment. As Gallistel notes: "In short, the rat has a map in the ordinary sense of the term, a Euclidian (distance- and angle-preserving) representation of the relative positions of the points in its environment" (ibid., p. 5). Gallistel thinks that ant navigation has much in common with rat navigation as the following example serves to illustrate:

On the featureless Tunisian desert, a long-legged, fast-moving ant leaves the protection of the humid nest on a foraging expedition. It moves across the desert in tortuous loops, running first this way, then that, but gradually progressing ever further away from the life-sustaining humidity of the nest. Finally it finds the carcass of a scorpion, uses its strong pincers to gouge out a chunk nearly its own size, then turns to orient to within one or two degrees of the straight line between itself and the nest entrance, a one-millimeter-wide hole, 40 meters distant. It runs a straight line for 43 meters, holding its course by maintaining its angle to the sun. Three meters past the point at which it should have encountered the entrance, the ant abruptly breaks into the search pattern by which it eventually locates it. A witness to this homeward journey finds it hard to resist the inference that the ant on its search for food possessed at every moment a representation of its position relative to the entrance to the nest, a spatial representation that enabled it to compute the solar angle and the distance of the homeward journey from wherever it happened to encounter food. (Ibid., p. 1)

Gallistel uses the term "representation" in its mathematical sense. The brain represents aspects of its environment when there is a functioning isomorphism between an aspect of the environment and a brain process that adapts the animal's behavior to it. The computations in question are mathematical and the notion of modularity employed is due to Fodor. The exacting route taken by the ant back to its nest suggests, I think, breathtakingly effective means–end reasoning. Such reasoning issues in exacting routes to the nest because natural selection has provided the ant with conditional reasoning capacities that exemplify virtues such as simplicity and other abductive inferential qualities. That is, global abductive virtues supervene on such conditional reasoning in the sense that the reasoning exhibited displays virtues such as simplicity, coherence, and such. How else can we explain the computational and representational abilities of such otherwise uncomplicated species as the ant?

But notice that the sort of abduction exhibited here is provided by natural selection. The means–end reasoning capacity of the ant is hardwired even if a particular use of that capacity is triggered by the proximal demands of its environment and its immediate need for food. But this is not an isolated case. Migratory birds also exhibit sophisticated behavior involving navigation to distant locales on a periodic basis that exploits the computational-representational framework that Gallistel defends. This suggests that much abductive work is evidenced in the process of natural selection and has as output, means–end reasoning structures that become encoded as modules in various species. If this is even close to the mark, then Fodor is right to emphasize the role of abduction in cognitive affairs. But it isn't explicit, occurrent, transparent-to-the-cognizer abduction that occurs. Rather, it is subdoxastic, evolutionary abduction that predominates by means of natural selection. This crucial point, I think, radically changes the nature of the massive modularity debate.

Spatial Reorientation

Let's take another example. An interesting study by Hermer and Spelke (1996) points the way to clarifying matters concerning knowledge of spatial reorientation. Aside from the cheater detection module, Cosmides and

Tooby's flagship example of a domain-specific, computational module, the spatial reorientation module is their second-best exemplar of their notion of a module. It would appear that both adult rats and young children spatially reorient themselves by appeal to an innate, informationally encapsulated, task-specific, modular, computational mechanism (Cheng 1986b; Cheng and Gallistel 1984). This mechanism appeals to the large-scale shape of the environment but not to the nongeometric properties of the environment, such as the color of a wall, the patterning on a box, or the categorical identity of an object. Instead, only geometric properties of the room, for example, length of a wall and angles, were appealed to for purposes of spatial reorientation. In contrast, adult humans appeal to both geometric and nongeometric properties of environments to reorient themselves with respect to the location of a hidden object. The authors suggest that the appeal to nongeometric properties to facilitate reorientation may be a late development in humans in one of two ways. Either humans become more flexible (and so less modular or task-specific) by overcoming the limitations of only appealing to geometric factors during development or the original geometric process may persist over cognitive development but new processes are added on. As they say:

[O]ur studies suggest there is a core cognitive process for representing the shape of the surrounding environment and for using this representation to compute one's own position within the environment. Operating beneath the level of conscious awareness, this process appears to contribute importantly to our sense, as adults, of where we are. As with the systems of knowledge underlying human language, number, reasoning about objects, and social understanding, the core properties of this system of geometric knowledge appear to emerge early in life and to be conserved over human development. In distinction to some of these other knowledge systems, the system of geometric knowledge may have emerged early in mammalian evolution, and its central features appear to be found in other mammals (see Gallistel and Gelman 1992 for parallel claims about the system of knowledge of number). (Hermer and Spelke 1996, p. 229)

The authors go on to suggest that common cognitive processes are to be expected across species especially when species are compared at early points in ontogeny. As they note: "Natural selection tends to operate not by effecting fundamental changes in pre-existing, adaptive traits but by conserving those traits and building new processes on top of them (Ridley, 1993). Evolutionary changes therefore tend to be implemented late in an organism's development, when they are less apt to disrupt other viable processes (Gould, 1992; Ridley, 1993). Cognitive capacities are likely to follow these general rules" (Hermer and Spelke 1996, p. 230). Gabriel Segal (1996) has called such changes "terminal additions." A consequence of this developmental picture is that the human ability to extend our knowledge into areas for which our biology has not prepared us can be better studied using a two-step procedure. First, work at understanding early-developing, task-specific mechanisms and; second, study how further cognitive processes are built on top of the initial ones to overcome their limitations.

2.11   Epistemic Implications

The spatial reorientation module is interesting for many reasons. Notice that spatial reorientation requires that we extract geometric and nongeometric information about the environment, locate ourselves in that environment, and then act to find a hidden object. In that process, we find input modules, output modules, and a module that connects those modules. All of this seems to be achieved without appeal to transparent, occurrent beliefs. However, it should be noted that adult human subjects showed some awareness that they were appealing to nongeometric processes in order to find keys "in the corner just to the left of the blue wall" in an otherwise white rectangular room. In contrast, in cases where only geometric properties were available, for example, there was no blue wall, subjects showed no awareness of their own appeal to geometric properties. Of course, showing some awareness of nongeometric properties does not entail that adult humans are engaging in explicit abductive inference here. Certainly, Hermer and Spelke would deny that explicit abductive inference occurs in such cases.

I think something like the model shown in figure 2.1 captures the situation. Notice that the NRA model explains how abduction figures in our cognitive economy. Spatial reorientation allows for a Gallistelian computational-representational framework involving subdoxastic representations that figure in means–end reasoning modules. The idea is that abduction through natural selection selects for means–end reasoning modules that produce belief sets that satisfy global desiderata. In the case of ants, they arrive at accurate representations of their environment that allow computations to take place resulting in effective behavior. In effect, mother nature is the ultimate abductive reasoner. Abductive reasoning of the sort I am considering supervenes on local computational modules. The triggering of such

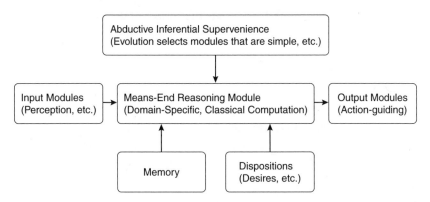

Figure 2.1
NRA: Nonreflective architecture (subdoxastic, computational-representational framework).

means–end reasoning modules by environmental cues and the dispositions of the organism may seem to require thought. The effects of natural selection are often like that. But none of this requires that abduction is explicit or that reflective thought is involved. On Gallistel's picture, neither ants nor rats nor humans need to engage in any reflective reasoning to complete the complex computations required for finding a hidden object after spatial reorientation, returning to a nest, or migrating to a different continent—nor do they need to for a myriad of other goals. In the face of this, it would not be surprising if cheater detection also did not require explicit abductive inference. Nothing that I am aware of in the literature on cheater detection indicates otherwise. The moral is that much goes on beneath the surface.

So, let me respond directly to Fodor's concern that a massively modular mind cannot explain abductive inference. In the first place, Cosmides and Tooby deny that the mind is composed entirely of local, computational processors. They allow that some aspects of cognition may well be carried out by nonmodular, domain-general abilities, for example, a bayesian inductive ability. In the second place, I think that a great deal of cognitive activity that looks like explicit abductive inference is really nothing of the sort. It is means–end reasoning by local, computational processors that were forged in the crucible of evolution by natural selection. Often, such reasoning produces sets of beliefs that exemplify global, abductive properties. This is because nonexplicit abductive inference supervenes on such local, computational processors in the sense that such processors were selected for exactly because they generate belief sets that satisfy abductive constraints. It follows that a kind of abductive inference can be manifest in a massively modular mind.

2.12   Conclusion

In the end, Fodor's position is much closer to the views of Cosmides and Tooby than one might have thought. Fodor attacks an extreme version of the massive modularity hypothesis that Cosmides and Tooby, in fact, do not accept. Hence, there remains good reason to think that the mind almost works the way that Cosmides and Tooby suggest it does. In chapter 3, I focus on the connection between falsity and representation. After canvasing several solutions to the disjunction problem, I attempt to provide a new account of misrepresentation. Representation, it turns out, is connected by way of evolution to falsity.

3 Misrepresentation and Massive Modularity

In this chapter, I argue that the "gap theory" solves the disjunction problem. Although Fodor's asymmetric dependence account of misrepresentation is on the right track in that it picks out a necessary condition for misrepresentation, it needs to be biologized in order to provide sufficient conditions for misrepresentation. Dretske and Millikan provide biologized accounts of misrepresentation, but they fail to solve the disjunction problem. The gap theory explains why Fodor's account is correct where it is correct. Unlike Dretske and Millikan's accounts, it provides biologically sufficient conditions for the explanation of misrepresentation. Hence, the gap theory extracts what is correct from earlier theories and forges those aspects into a better account.

3.1 The Disjunction Problem

Minimally, causal theorists hold that, in cases where a predicative expression ("Deer") is thought of an object of predication (a deer), the symbol tokenings denote their causes, and the symbol types express the property "whose instantiations reliably cause their tokenings" (Fodor 1987, p. 99). In the successful case, my uttering "deer" says of a deer that it is one. The idea was that reliable causation would be counterfactual supporting in the sense that the property deer does cause the tokening of "deer," and that this property would cause the tokening of "deer" if the property were instantiated. The idea behind the causal theory is that such nomological relations determine the semantic interpretation of mental symbols. The central problem for the causal theory of representation was to give an account of misrepresentation. A problem for many solutions to the misrepresentation problem is the disjunction problem. According to the crude causal theory of representation, D reliably causes tokenings of "D." As such, it looks like the condition governing what it means for D to be represented by "D" is identical to the condition for such a token being true. If so, it is impossible to get falsity or unveridicality into the picture. Now one might think that D-caused "D" tokenings are veridical and E-caused "D" tokenings are unveridical. Hence, there is no problem here.

But this will not wash. The existence of E-caused "D" tokenings establishes the fact that the causal dependence of "D" tokenings on Ds is imperfect. It would seem that "D" tokenings are reliably caused by the disjunctive property of being (D or E). But if "D" expresses the property (D or E), then E-caused "D" tokenings are veridical and we have no theory of misrepresentation. That is the disjunction problem. There are two kinds of cases that a viable causal theory of content has to acknowledge, as Fodor put it: "the case where the content of the symbol is disjunctive ('A' expresses the property of being (A or B)) and the case where the content of the symbol is not disjunctive and some of the tokenings are false ('A' expresses the property of being A, and B-caused 'A' tokenings are false)" (Fodor 1987, p. 102). The crude causal theory of content is unable to distinguish between these cases since it always "assigns disjunctive content to symbols whose causally sufficient conditions are themselves disjoint" (ibid.).

A problem that is closely related to the disjunction problem is what we might call "Quine's problem." Quine's problem is to determine belief content in the case where verbal behavior results in indeterminacy of translation. In the case of radical translation abroad, the field linguist in the wild hears the native utter "gavagai" in the presence of a rabbit but it is unclear as to whether the native is referring to rabbit parts, rabbit stages, rabbits, and so on. Quine famously suggested that there are too many adequate interpretations in such cases.[1] Quine also thinks that indeterminacy occurs on the home front where translation between two known languages occurs.

In the context of potential error, a slightly different problem emerges: do we attribute to the native a very specific but false belief, or a less specific but true belief? For instance, the native might just be truly asserting that there is an animal in the vicinity when he says "gavagai," or he might be referring to a particular bone in the left foot of a particular type of rabbit. This bone, however, does not exist in that type of rabbit. As such, what the native asserts is false. We can make most of the utterances of a foreign speaker come out false if we adopt the latter approach to assigning content to beliefs. But what is the correct approach—or is there one? I will call this "Dretske's problem" since he articulated it clearly in a 1989 paper entitled "The Need to Know."

Of course, Davidson and Dennett addressed Dretske's problem by invoking principles of rationality (though these principles were not offered as a solution to Dretske's problem, since Dretske's paper was published after their work).[2] Roughly, one must, in the first instance, take most of a speaker's beliefs to be true and most of a speaker's inferences to be valid. Otherwise, it will be impossible to assign any interpretation to a speaker's verbal output or assign any content to their mental states. (See Stich 1990, p. 11.) Whether the Davidson–Dennett thesis is correct is an issue that I will not directly address in what follows. But I will consider Quine's and Dretske's problems later as we move toward a solution to the disjunction problem. The disjunction problem is a semantic issue, whereas the other two problems are epistemological problems. It will turn out that we can address the epistemological problems by resolving the semantic problem. In order to set the stage for my positive account, I now want to briefly rehearse some attempts to solve the disjunction problem.

3.2 Dretske's First Solution

In *Knowledge and the Flow of Information*, Dretske offered what became known as the learning gambit to explain misrepresentation. Dretske developed an account of information that drew its inspiration from Shannon's information theory to argue that the central semantic relation is one that holds between two events when one of them transmits information about the other. The mathematical theory of information or communication theory measures the amount of information in a given situation and how much of this information is available for transmission to other points. The theory is purely quantitative, dealing simply with amounts of information. It identifies the amount of information generated by an event with the reduction in uncertainty or the elimination of possibilities represented by that event.

For instance, if we need to choose a person to do a task from a group of eight people and adopt a coin-tossing method to decide who will get the task, then information theory suggests a way to measure the information

associated with this selection. We divide the group into two groups of four
and a coin is flipped. This reduces the contestants to four, out of which two
groups are formed, and a coin is tossed again. The final two contestants repeat the procedure and the "winner" is determined. Three coin tosses determine the winner. This is the number of binary decisions needed to reduce
eight alternatives to one. Information theorists think this is the correct way
to measure the amount of information involved in this case. As Dretske
notes: "It takes three binary digits (bits), one binary digit (0 or 1) for each
flip of the coin (letting 1=heads, 0=tails), to completely specify the reduction of eight possibilities to one. The amount of information associated
with the fact that Herman was selected is 3 bits" (1980, p. 5). Eventually
Dretske offers an account of misrepresentation based on his interpretation
of information theory as follows. As Fodor quotes Dretske:

"In the learning situation special care is taken to see that incoming signals have an in-
tensity, a strength, sufficient unto delivering the required piece of information to the
learning subject. . . . Such precautions are taken in the learning situation . . . in order
to ensure that an internal structure is developed with . . . the information that s is
F. . . . But once we have meaning, once the subject has articulated a structure that is
selectively sensitive to information about the F-ness of things, instances of this structure, tokens of this type, can be triggered by signals that lack the appropriate piece of
information. . . . We [thus] have a case of misrepresentation—a token of a structure
with a false content. We have, in a word, meaning without truth" (KFI, 194–195; em-
phases Dretske's). (Fodor 1987, pp. 102–103)

Dretske's notion of information is that of counterfactual-supporting correlation: events of type "A" carry information about events of type A to the
extent that the latter sorts of event are reliably causally responsible for
events of the former sort. Information essentially involves a particular sort
of correlation. The problem is that it looks as though there is no such thing
as a miscorrelation, hence no such thing as misinformation. Dretske's solution is to enforce a strict distinction between what happens during the
learning period and what happens after the learning period. Dretske needs
a strict, principled distinction if he is to explain misrepresentation, since
there must be such a thing as a correct representation as a logical precondition for error. Otherwise, there would be no way to tell accurate from inac-
curate representation. The notion of a learning period was intended to
capture exactly such a strict, principled difference.

The problem with this account, according to Fodor, and I think he is
right, is that anything that happens after the learning period can happen

during the learning period. Therefore, there is no principled distinction between what happens after and what happens during the learning period. As
such, disjunctive properties can arise during the learning period. Suppose
John learns that "A" tokenings refer to As in the learning period. After the
learning period, John mistakes a B for an "A." Counterfactually, John could
have done the same thing during the learning period. If so, then (A or B)
would have caused "A" tokenings. As Fodor notes: "So we have the same old
problem back again. If 'A's are correlated with (A ∨ B)'s, then the content of
a tokening of 'A' is that A ∨ B. So a B-caused 'A' tokening isn't false. So we're
still in want of a way out of the disjunction problem" (1987, p. 104). For this
reason, Dretske's solution to the disjunction problem fails.

3.3   A Teleological Solution

Dennis Stampe's "Toward a Causal Theory of Linguistic Representation" (in
French, Uehling, and Wettstein 1977) and an article of Fodor's entitled "Psychosemantics" (in Lycan 1990) offered an alternative solution to the disjunction problem. The idea was that in optimal circumstances, As would
cause "A" tokenings, even if, in the actual situation, (A ∨ B)s cause "A" tokenings. On this view, a symbol expresses its "optimal" property in the
sense that it expresses the property that would causally control its tokening
in optimal circumstances. But trouble develops in the context of providing
an account of optimal circumstances. "Optimal circumstances" have to be
explicated naturalistically. That is, the explication of "optimal circumstances" must proceed in terms that are not semantical or intentional. The
idea was to appeal to teleology to explicate "optimal circumstances." Optimal circumstances are the ones in which the mechanisms that mediate symbol tokenings are functioning "as they are supposed to."

  In the case of beliefs, these mechanisms would be mechanisms of belief
fixation. In short: "The teleology of the cognitive mechanisms determines
the optimal conditions for belief fixation, and the optimal conditions for
belief fixation determine the content of beliefs" (Fodor 1987, p. 105). Only
As cause "A" tokenings in optimal circumstances, so that when the mechanisms of belief fixation are working properly, the beliefs produced will be
true. But how do we know that the mechanisms of belief fixation are designed to always deliver truth? They might be designed to repress truths,
truths the acknowledgement of which would be unbearable. It might be

argued that beliefs that are merely useful for survival and reproduction need not be true. In this way, true beliefs would come apart from the merely useful beliefs supplied by mechanisms of belief fixation that natural selection has supplied for us. For instance, we might believe that we have a moral obligation to care for our sister's offspring, where, in fact, the actual biological cause of our behavior is that we have a 25 percent genetic investment in our sister's offspring. Yet, we persist in believing that we are taking care of "little Johnny" out of a sense of duty. In fact, Stich drove this home in his 1983 book, *From Folk Psychology to Cognitive Science*. Fodor accepted the point and has continued to be wary of optimality claims concerning evolution ever since. According to Fodor, explicating optimality in terms of teleology and teleology in terms of evolution is a "dead theory" (Fodor 1990, p. 77).

3.4 Fodor's Asymmetric Dependence Account

Fodor thinks that the right approach involves the counterfactual properties of the causal relations between As and "A" tokenings, and Bs and "A" tokenings. He argues that falsehoods are ontologically dependent on truths, but not vice versa. That is, one can make the error of confusing a cow with a horse only once one has the notion of a horse. So that if I see a cow and say "horse," that error is an error only in virtue of the existence of the independent semantic relation between "horse" tokenings and horses. Falsehoods are dependent on truths, but truths are not dependent on falsehoods. Hence, since "horse" does mean horse, the "fact that horses cause me to say 'horse' does not depend upon there being a semantic—or, indeed, any—connection between 'horse' tokenings and cows" (Fodor 1987, p. 108). The causal connection between cows and "horse" tokenings is asymmetrically dependent on the causal connection between horses and "horse" tokenings. A false or wild tokening can now be picked out in terms of the necessary condition: "B-caused 'A' tokenings are wild only if they are asymmetrically dependent upon non-B-caused 'A' tokenings" (ibid.).

I think this account of misrepresentation is very good. It succeeds in picking out a necessary semantic dependency relation that all misrepresentations bear to accurate representations. This was clearly an advance over earlier attempts, such as Dretske's and Stampe's, at solving the disjunction problem, for it crystallized the point that a necessary condition on any adequate solution to the disjunction problem must have the result that misrepresentation be logically parasitic on accurate representation. In that sense, it parallels Peter Unger's point in epistemology that any adequate account of knowledge must have the result that knowledge is nonaccidental. Of course, spelling out what nonaccidentality comes to is difficult and also has its parallel in our case. This is because Fodor's constraint needs to be naturalized in order to be ambulatory and that is no easy task. The point is that in both cases a constraint has been laid down that is very plausible, but that constraint does not constitute an account of the concept under scrutiny but a condition that any such account must satisfy. In one sense the account is naturalized: it avoids semantic and intentional talk.

But in at least one other important sense of "naturalized," the asymmetric dependence account of misrepresentation is not a naturalized account: the account does not clarify how error occurs in the natural world. One could be aware of Fodor's necessary condition on wild tokenings and be aware of instantiations of that necessary condition in the natural order, and still something would be missing. What would be missing would be an account of the deep, biologically sufficient conditions that give rise to error. What is needed is an account of misrepresentation that invokes the systematic categories of biology. Anything less will be superficial from the scientific standpoint. For instance, if I call a cow a "horse" then I will make an error. "Horse" is a wild token in this case. I have satisfied Fodor's necessary condition for such wild tokens and the case does exist in nature. However, I have not succeeded in explaining how wild tokens occur in the wild in any systematic, biologically satisfactory way. Fodor explicitly fails to provide sufficient conditions concerning the nature of wild tokens. Some will say that it is not the job of a semantic theory to provide an account of the deep, biologically sufficient conditions that give rise to error. It may be that a full account of our cognitive abilities would require such an account, but a theory that specifies necessary conditions for a mental state to have a particular meaning need not do this.[3] My response is to insist that one must accept the fact that accurate representation and misrepresentation are relational notions. They involve the relation between a representation and what it represents. In turn, the nature of that relation depends on the representer and her cognitive abilities. For this reason, providing a semantic theory inevitably involves us in assessing the role of our cognitive abilities as they have an impact on the world. Since that impact is realized by virtue of our biology, it follows that we need an account of the deep, biologically sufficient conditions that give rise to error.

Presumably, the role of our cognitive abilities in representing states of the world is profound. Even some of those who champion a correspondence theory of truth (such as Alvin Goldman in *Epistemology and Cognition* [1986], pp. 152–156) admit that there is a Kantian contructivist element involved in it. That is, we create versions or conceptions of the external world that our experience confirms or fails to confirm. In that limited sense, truth is constructed. By analogy, jeans are constructed by humans, whereas facts about the world determine whether they fit an individual. Any deep explanation of the sort required for an adequate semantic theory must clarify the sufficient biological conditions that give rise to, and the role of, our cognitive abilities in the construction of semantic content. Our semantic theory is, and must be, inextricably interwoven with our psychology and biology. Meaning does not pop out of thin air, divorced from the humans that produce it. *Pace* Fodor, we need to biologize the notion of misrepresentation if we think that it is important to naturalize content and provide an adequate explanatory account of it. Fortunately, Millikan and Dretske attempt to provide the appropriate biologization of error that I seek by developing a teleosemantic or teleofunctional account of what determines the semantic contents of inner representations.

3.5   Dretske's Magnetosome Case

Dretske attempts, in "Misrepresentation" (1986) and *Explaining Behavior* (1988), to show that there are biological systems that have as their function to "represent" or "indicate" states of the environment. For this reason, his view is sometimes called "indicator semantics." Dretske argues that these functions have been selected in evolutionary history because they played an important information-gathering role that was crucial to satisfying a biological need, or they have been selected through a learning process for a similar reason. Dretske's key example concerns the magnetotactic systems of certain northern hemisphere bacteria. Such systems contain tiny magnets that pull toward geomagnetic north. This causes them to go down, away from the surface of the water, toward regions of lesser oxygen. Oxygen is toxic for these bacteria. The problem is to determine which of these things it is the function of the magnetosome to indicate. That is, is it the function of the magnetosome to represent (1) geomagnetic north, (2) magnetic north, or (3) nontoxic, oxygen-free water? Dretske claims the answer is indeterminate: "this primitive sensory mechanism is, after all, functioning perfectly well when it leads its possessor into a toxic environment" (Dretske 1986, p. 29). What the magnetosome needs to have represented is "nontoxic, oxygen-free water," but clearly the device is a magnetotactic device, not a chemotactic device. Since that is the case, the needed function does not correspond to the actual device that the bacteria possess.

Dretske is acutely aware of the problem. As he notes: "The problem we face is the problem of accounting for the misrepresentational capacities of a system without doing so by artificially inflating the natural functions of such a system" (1986, p. 32). Regrettably, Dretske has no solution to this problem given the magnetotactic device that the bacteria employ, and so he concludes that misrepresentation cannot occur in bacteria. But clearly this is an inadequate response to give when we induce the bacteria toward the surface of the water with a bar magnet and it dies. The evidence trumps theory. The result, I think, is that Dretske's account fails to explain how the needed biological function is selected that allows the bacteria to gravitate toward nontoxic, oxygen-free water, and so he has no account of function and so no account of malfunction. As such, he cannot explain how misrepresentation naturally occurs. But we should heed his warning; we must not artificially inflate the natural functions of a system in order to provide an account of misrepresentation. As we shall see, Millikan commits this sin by invoking the notion of a representation consumer.

3.6   Millikan's Proper Function Account

Millikan (1993) offers what seems to be an improvement over Dretske's account of misrepresentation in "Biosemantics" and "Compare and Contrast Dretske, Fodor, and Millikan on Teleosemantics." She invokes the notion of a representation consumer in order to suggest that the magnetosome needs to represent "nontoxic, oxygen-free water." As she notes:

Representation consumers are devices that have been designed (in the first instances, at least) by a selection process to cooperate with a certain representation producer. The producer likewise has been designed to match the consumer. What the consumer's function is, what it is supposed to effect in responding as it does to the representations that it consumes, could be anything at all. It may have numerous alternative functions. It may also be but one of the many consumer systems that use representations made by the same producer. The consumer operates, of course, after the producer does, and a full explanation of how the consumer has historically managed to perform its function or functions—in Millikan's terminology, a full "Normal explanation for proper performance" of its function—would include that the producer first performed its function properly, and it would include an explanation of how the producer's function has historically been accomplished. (Millikan 1993, p. 126)

As a consumer of representations, the bacteria need to represent "nontoxic, oxygen-free water," but as a representation-producer the magnetosome simply produces the representation "geomagnetic north" or even "magnetic north." In the environment in question, the representation-producer produces a representation that is then consumed by the representation-consumer. Misrepresentation or error gets into the picture when, for instance, a magnet is held above the water. In this sort of case, the bacteria would move up in the water and die from the toxic, oxygen-rich water. The representation-producer does not make the error because it can make no errors (Dretske is right about that); the representation-consumer makes the error. It thinks (metaphorically speaking) that it is moving toward "nontoxic, oxygen-free water" but is mistaken because the representation-producer is not representing geomagnetic north properly, though it is representing magnetic north properly.

The difference, of course, is that the environment has been rigged such that magnetic north is where the hand-held magnet is located above the water rather than where it normally is, deeper in the water toward geomagnetic north. Dretske's mistake (and the mistake of all causal theorists), according to Millikan, is to focus on the representation-producer only and ignore the representation-consumer. The consumer errs when the proper function that was historically selected for fails to go off in the way that it historically did. Misrepresentation or error, in effect, is malfunction. The proper function of some device need not always, or even usually, perform successfully. As she notes: "being reliable can't be the function of any teleofunctional item for the easy reason that no item effects its own reliability. Reliability always depends on the dependability of external factors, on the prevalence or rarity of normal conditions for proper performance" (Millikan 1993, p. 130).

It seems doubtful that Dretske or anyone would argue that the function of any teleofunctional item is to be reliable or that reliability tout court is a viable notion. Of course, functions describe the recurring, causal interactions of physically realized objects, and reliability has to be relative to a context of some sort, for example, the actual world. To think otherwise is to deeply misunderstand causal theorists. At any rate Millikan, unlike Dretske, denies that there must be a reliable nomic connection between representation and represented or between cause and effect for a function to exist. Yet, it would seem that the connection between representation and represented is reliable in the case of the representation-producer in the bacteria. That causal relation is near perfect. What is unreliable but often successful is the instantiation of the proper function of the representation-consumer in the bacteria. About this fact, Millikan is surely right. But do such representation-consumers actually exist, or are they merely philosophical figments of Millikan's imagination? Can we really just posit whatever we need to explain the facts of what, ultimately, is an empirical story? No; as tempting as the idea of a representation-consumer is, it would seem unreasonable to grant her complete freedom here, absent an empirical grounding for the story. Millikan needs empirical evidence to support the notion of a representation-consumer, not just-so stories, and this she fails to provide.

Second, has Millikan simply committed the artificial inflation error concerning proper functions that Dretske warned us to avoid? Has Millikan accounted for the misrepresentational capacities of the bacteria by artificially inflating the nature of its natural functions? I think she has. First, she invents the notion of a representation-consumer and then she gives this consumer the capacity to err. In reality, she commits two errors by (1) creating ontology where there is none, that is, the representation-consumer, and (2) artificially inflating the natural functions of a system, that is, bacteria.[4] Millikan artificially inflates the natural functions of the bacteria in the sense that the internal device that the bacterium employs is a magnetotactic device, not a chemotactic device. But the representation-consumer, on her view, represents the notion of nontoxic, oxygen-free water. This makes the device in question a chemotactic device and so inflates the natural functions of the bacteria. In what follows, however, I will attempt to improve on Millikan's account of misrepresentation by avoiding errors (1) and (2). At the same time, I will try to provide an account of misrepresentation that, unlike Dretske's account, succeeds.

3.7   Two Kinds of Error

Misrepresentation, or error, is not uncommon in the natural order.[5] Humans, for instance, make visual perception errors as with the Müller-Lyer illusion. We also make a variety of inductive and deductive inferential errors as has been ably demonstrated over the past thirty years by Kahneman and Tversky, Nisbett and Ross, Wason, Johnson-Laird, Cosmides and Tooby, Gigerenzer and Hug, and many other psychologists. One also thinks here of the false belief task and other representational errors that have been intensively studied by psychologists working on child development, such as Gopnik and Wellman, Carey and Spelke, Harris, Leslie, and many others. I think all errors can be sorted into two types: competence errors and performance errors.[6] I begin with the overarching competence/performance error distinction on the assumption that misrepresentation constitutes a subset of these broader categories of error. My view is that misrepresentation can be fully understood only within this broader framework.

The competence/performance distinction has its origins in Chomsky's discussion of an internally represented grammar of a natural language. On Chomsky's view such a grammar consists in an integrated set of generative rules and principles that result in an infinite number of claims about the language. For each sentence in the language, the grammar entails that it is grammatical; for each ambiguous sentence, the grammar entails that it is ambiguous, and so on. Our linguistic intuitions access, nonconsciously, our innate, internally represented grammar. For this reason, such intuitions are evidence for linguists pursuing the nature of the grammar. But linguistic intuitions are not an infallible source for determining the grammar since the production of such intuitions depends on other cognitive mechanisms, such as those subserving perception, motivation, attention, short-term memory, and many others. Hence, these other mechanisms rather than the grammar may lead judgments of grammaticality astray. For instance, there is evidence suggesting that short-term memory cannot handle center-embedded structures. Our internally represented grammars may entail that the following sentence is grammatical:

What what what he wanted cost would buy in Germany was amazing.

Here it seems our intuitions tell us that this sentence is not grammatical. The internally represented grammar constitutes one's linguistic competence, while the judgments and sentences that one produces constitute one's linguistic performance. When one's judgments or the sentences produced differ from those dictated by grammatical competence, we say that the subject committed a performance error.

Cognitive scientists interested in reasoning have suggested that there are many parallels between the linguistic case and the reasoning case. In both cases there is a spontaneous and mostly unconscious processing of an infinite number of inputs. People are able to understand and draw inferences from many sentences. Moreover, they are able to make intuitive judgments about validity and probability in reasoning just as they are able to make judgments about grammaticality and ambiguity in linguistics. For these reasons, it has been suggested that there is a mechanism underlying our ability to reason just as there is a mechanism underlying our ability to process language. As such, the claim is that there is an integrated set of rules and principles of reasoning, an underlying psycho-logic, which is accessed and relied on when people draw inferences or make judgments about inferences that they make (Samuels, Stich, and Tremoulet 1998, pp. 139–140). The processes and principles would not, for the most part, be accessible to consciousness. Moreover, people's inferences and judgments would not be infallible since, as with grammar, the psycho-logic must interact with other cognitive mechanisms subserving attention, motivation, short-term memory, and such. The result is that these other mechanisms can cause performance errors: inferences or judgments that are incompatible with one's psycho-logic or reasoning competence. Where the error is due to the psycho-logic itself, we have a competence error. One can imagine the linguistic distinction and the reasoning distinction, together with the related errors, generalizing to other cognitive mechanisms. The result would be a universal competence/performance error distinction.

The idea is that any output error that is caused by the central mechanism subserving the type of output in question constitutes a competence error. In contrast, any error caused by an enabling cognitive mechanism that works alongside the central mechanism constitutes a performance error. To be sure, it may be very difficult to distinguish matters that concern a central mechanism from those that concern enabling mechanisms. But, on the assumption that psychologists can clarify the issue in particular cases, we would have a robust universal competence/performance distinction in hand. As it turns out, I do not think that humans possess a domain-general, content-neutral, underlying psycho-logic; I believe, with Cosmides and Tooby, that the mind is massively modular. But the point still stands: errors caused by a module that subserves a particular type of inference will be competence errors. Errors caused by an enabling cognitive mechanism in the same context will be performance errors.

A second distinction concerns modular versus nonmodular errors. This distinction cuts across the competence/performance distinction. Hence, there can be modular competence errors and nonmodular competence errors. However, I will accept the massive modularity hypothesis of Cosmides and Tooby and argue that the mind is largely composed of computational modules. A module, on the view that I will push, is a computational device that takes as inputs domain-specific information. Such computational devices are the legacy of our Pleistocene forebears. They are innate devices that were selected for in response to the adaptive problems that our ancestors faced. Cosmides and Tooby explain the idea:

> Our cognitive architecture resembles a confederation of hundreds or thousands of functionally dedicated computers (often called modules) designed to solve the adaptive problems endemic to our hunter-gatherer ancestors. Each of these devices has its own agenda and imposes its own exotic organization on different fragments of the world. There are specialized systems for grammar induction, for face recognition, for dead reckoning, for construing objects and for recognizing emotions from the face. There are mechanisms to detect animacy, eye direction, and cheating. There is a "theory of mind" module . . . a variety of social inference modules . . . and a multitude of other elegant machines. (Cosmides and Tooby 1995, p. xiv)

Each such module has a proper function that reliably produces outputs that helped our ancestors negotiate their environment.

Following Wright, I will offer this analysis of function:

> The function of X is Z means:
> (a) X is there because it does Z,
> (b) Z is a consequence (or result) of X's being there. (Wright 1998, p. 71)

"Because" has its ordinary, conversational, causal-explanatory sense here, as in "He was hungry because his stomach had contracted," as opposed to the intensional sense of "because." As such, it has etiological force in that the existence of X is explained as a function of its doing Z. To say that "because" has etiological force is to say that we are appealing to the evolutionary history or genesis of X. "Consequence" is intended asymmetrically: Z is a consequence of X and not vice versa. Condition (b) picks out functional etiologies from nonfunctional etiologies, as when we say that the function of oxygen in human blood streams is to provide energy in oxidation reactions and not to combine with hemoglobin (Wright 1998, p. 69). Nevertheless, oxygen does combine with hemoglobin. That oxygen provides energy is a functional etiological fact; that oxygen combines with hemoglobin is a nonfunctional etiological fact. So condition (b) picks out functional from nonfunctional etiologies in the sense that Z (energy) is a consequence or result of X (oxygen) in the human blood stream and not vice versa, whereas it isn't the case that Z (hemoglobin) is a consequence or result of X (oxygen).

In short, the evolutionary function of oxygen is to create energy, not to combine with hemoglobin, even though it is a contingent fact that oxygen does combine with hemoglobin. The notion of consequence or result in condition (b) is intended to mark this important difference. For Millikan, a "proper" function is, then, the function for which the trait was selected in evolutionary history. What is added to this, by Cosmides and Tooby, is the idea that such etiological, proper functions apply to modules and that such functions "reliably" produce results like that for which they were selected. Millikan, in contrast, denies that such proper functions must be reliable. Beaver slaps, on her view, often fail to genuinely indicate danger though that is the proper function of such slaps. I will later side with Cosmides and Tooby on this point.

In contrast, a nonmodular account of the mind would suggest that we employ domain-general capacities in the sense that reasoning, for instance, might be thought to range over informational inputs of various kinds, for example, those emanating from perceptual, auditory, or other sources. Fodor's notion of a central processor that uses a general reasoning capability to process information from various modular input systems is one example of a nonmodular processor. It should be noted that Fodor's conception of a module is different from Cosmides and Tooby's conception of the same.[7]

I, following Sperber, will call the environment within which a proper function is selected for its "proper domain," as opposed to the "actual domain" (Sperber 1994, p. 51). Hence, the domain in which a proper function of a computational module was selected for constitutes its proper domain. The domain in which the computational module that was selected for now operates is its actual domain. Of course, the gap between the proper domain and the actual domain may be considerable. The result is that a module that was reliable in its proper domain or the environment of evolutionary adaptation (EEA) may no longer be reliable in the actual domain or actual environment (AE). (See Cosmides and Tooby 1994.) A central claim that I want to make is that misrepresentation or error, of all kinds, is a part of the process that leads to malfunction. "Malfunction," on the other hand, constitutes a case where the proper function of a module fails to go off as it did in the EEA. In such cases, the AE is sufficiently distinct from the EEA, such that the instantiation of the proper function is not successful. In short, the differences between the EEA and the AE can explain most cases of modular error.

To be sure, malfunction can also occur for other reasons, such as fatigue or other environmental factors outside the control of the cognizer. And, to the extent that part of the mind is likely to be nonmodular, a different analysis will be required to handle such cases. Note also that there is an asymmetric dependence of malfunctions relative to the proper functioning of a module. That is, the idea of malfunction makes sense only relative to the idea of the proper functioning of a module. In this sense, Fodor is correct to say that error is asymmetrically dependent on truth whereas truth is not asymmetrically dependent on falsity. Even if there were no errors, there could be truth. But the reverse does not hold: if there were no truths, there could be no errors. In nature this logical point is cashed out empirically as the fact that there can be no malfunctions without proper functions, though there could be proper functions without malfunctions. Where belief is involved in nature, error presupposes truth. More generally, malfunction or unsuccessful activity presupposes the notion of correct proper function instantiation or successful activity. In all cases, malfunction is parasitic on the correct instantiation of proper function (but not vice versa).

The account of error that I will defend takes its starting point from a suggestion by Cosmides and Tooby in their article entitled "Origins of domain-specificity: The evolution of functional organization." As they note:

> With relatives as with so many other things, what counts as adaptive error differs from domain to domain. In the sexual domain, error = sex with kin. In the helping domain, error = not helping kin given the appropriate envelope of circumstances. In cooperative exchanges, error = being cheated, which involves paying a cost without receiving the benefit to which this entitles you. When a lion is looking for lunch, error = offering yourself as an appetizer. Because what counts as the wrong thing to do differs from domain to domain, there must be as many domain-specific mechanisms as there are domains in which the definitions of successful behavioral outcomes are incommensurate. (Cosmides and Tooby 1994, p. 92)

Though the details of what counts as an error are domain specific, I think the characterization of error must be abstract (on condition that biological categories are invoked). I want to argue that the massive modularity hypothesis of Cosmides and Tooby, combined with an etiological, reliable proper function account of the computational processes that constitute such modules, can explain misrepresentation or error.[8] On my view, it will turn out that the disjunction problem can be resolved within the massive modularity account of cognitive architecture. One need only appeal to the malfunctioning of the relevant innate, domain-specific, computational processes. One advantage of this account is that it applies to all the modules of a massively modular mind and not just to cases of learning as with Dretske's account. To see more clearly how such an account might proceed, let's consider Dretske's magnetosome example.

3.8   Errors Ain't in the Head

Earlier I argued that Dretske's analysis of the magnetosome case failed because he has no way to explain the fact that the bacterium has made an error when it moves up in the water toward the bar magnet and dies. The proximal cause of the movement of the bacteria is the bar magnet held overhead. And, relative to that bar magnet, the magnetosome makes no error. Yet, the bacteria dies, so there is an error—but it is one Dretske cannot explain. Millikan's account appears to be an improvement in the sense that, by focusing on the representation-consumer, she can appeal to the crucial representation, namely, that the bacteria needs nontoxic, oxygen-free water and cannot acquire it because it links magnetic north with oxygen-free water. However, the situation is one where magnetic north is (abnormally) correlated with toxic, oxygen-rich water. So the bacteria dies. I suggested that Millikan could not just help herself to the notion of a representation-consumer. This is a notion that needs to be established empirically. It may be that cognitive ethology can deliver the evidence for this notion, but then it is up to Millikan to provide that evidence. Second, Millikan suggests that the representation-consumer represents nontoxic, oxygen-free water in the normal case, but it is exceedingly implausible to suppose that such a distal need is represented by anything in the bacteria. It may be that the bacteria needs such water, but it does not follow that it represents this in the sense that the magnetosome represents geomagnetic north. The bacteria would need a chemotactic device to represent nontoxic, oxygen-free water, and this it fails to possess.

My solution is to appeal to the idea of a proper domain/actual domain gap to explain error. Like Hume and Quine, I have a taste for desert landscapes when it comes to metaphysics. In the magnetosome case, the bacteria that has a bar magnet above it and dies is the victim of abnormal circumstances. Its response to the bar magnet results in disaster because the bar magnet has undermined the normal triggering device, geomagnetic north. The proper function of the magnetosome historically was to acquire nontoxic, oxygen-free water so as to facilitate survival and reproduction. The magnetosome did this, in successful cases, by representing geomagnetic north, because it is a magnetotactic device, not a chemotactic device. Geomagnetic north, in turn, correlated in the environment with nontoxic, oxygen-free water. As fate would have it, abnormal circumstances have led to error. The magnetosome misrepresents magnetic north as geomagnetic north. In this sense, misrepresentation is part of the process that leads to malfunction even though it is not the same thing as malfunction. The misrepresentation of geomagnetic north causes malfunction when the magnetosome moves upward in the water. The gap between the proper domain and the actual domain is too large. The result is that the proper function of the magnetosome cannot be realized and so it dies. More generally: there is an inverse relation between the proper/actual domain gap and the malfunction/proper function relation. Roughly, the greater the proper/actual gap, the lesser the likelihood that a module's proper function will operate successfully. Alternatively, the smaller the gap between the actual and proper domain, the greater the chances that the proper function of a module will operate successfully. Misrepresentation or error ain't in the head.

The deeper point to notice is that because externalism about meaning is true, mind–world connections result in meaning via generally reliable, proper functions. It is no surprise, then, that misrepresentation depends on mind–world connections going astray. How else could we have explained misrepresentation? We do not need to create representation-consumers to explain how error naturally occurs in the wild. All that is needed is to observe the facts with respect to how environments change. Of course, I do not intend to suggest that no errors occurred in the EEA; the Pleistocene were not perfect. The point is that error is a relative notion in the sense that it is contingently parasitic on what had been successful in the relevant EEA that one is comparing to the current AE.

Consider another case. Suppose there has been selection for a warning module in the proper domain of beavers. The module responds to threats from predators by causing a dominant beaver to slap the surface of the water. But now suppose that the actual domain no longer contains predators that would threaten the existence of beavers because the beavers live in Disney World in Florida. An artificial device constructed by a clever though slightly perverse engineer now triggers the warning module of these beavers. The idea is to simulate real-life conditions so that the patrons of Disney World can experience normal reactions by beavers in a "lifelike" setting. In particular, artificial elements of the natural habitat are created for the beavers, such as fake predators, taped sounds, and manmade "natural" environments. The result is that the beaver's warning module is constantly triggered by the actual environment, but the module is malfunctioning: no predators (other than businessmen) are in sight. Once again, it seems clear that the gap between the proper domain and the actual domain has caused malfunctions to occur in the warning module. The misrepresentation of danger has lead to fleeing behavior, and so the proper function of the warning module malfunctions. Once again, misrepresentation is part of the process that leads to malfunction.

Finally, consider Cosmides and Tooby's cheater detection module. This module functions in the context of social exchange contexts that involve a cost–benefit structure that is recognized as such by subjects. In such cases, reasoning performance is very good. Where no such cost–benefit structure is involved in a social exchange context, reasoning performance is considerably worse. Suppose that the proper domain where selection for the cheater detection module occurred always involved three elements: a social exchange context, a cost–benefit structure embedded in the social exchange context, and a recognition that a cost–benefit structure was involved by the relevant cognizers. Consider the well-known travel example concerning the Wason selection task (Cummins 1996). Deontic reasoning concerns what one may, ought, or must not do in a set of circumstances. Indicative reasoning concerns the epistemic status of factual or descriptive rules. It can be evaluated in terms of hypothesis testing, that is, testing the truth content of a rule in a particular set of circumstances. A deontic travel example is as follows. You pretend that you work for the Arizona transportation bureau, and it is your job to enforce a new law aimed at reducing air pollution due to car emissions. The law is "If you go to Phoenix, you must travel by train." You are shown four cards that have writing on both sides, but you see only one side. The cards say (respectively):

Phoenix   Tucson   Train   Car

Your task is to turn over all and only those cards necessary to determine whether the rule is being followed. Most people get the correct answer here and pick the "Phoenix" and "Car" cards, this is, the p and not-q cards. In this way, they usually reason in accord with the propositional calculus by using a violation-detecting strategy.

We can make this into an indicative conditional rule by removing the "must" from the conditional. It now reads: "If you go to Phoenix, you travel by train." Given the same four-card test, most subjects pick "Phoenix" and "Train" in this case, that is, p and q. Hence, a rule-confirming evidence strategy is employed. The point is that indicative rules result in this rule-confirming strategy whereas deontic rules result in a violation-detection strategy. The first strategy violates the propositional calculus, since the "Train" card does not have to be turned while the "Car" card does have to be turned. The second strategy does not violate the propositional calculus. Authors such as Denise Cummins, Gird Gigerenzer, Cosmides and Tooby, and others agree that an innate, domain-specific, cheater detection module is triggered by deontic reasoning formulations of the Wason selection task. If one wanted to construct a logically equivalent case to the Dretske bacteria example, it would go as follows. You would need an actual environment where the cheater detection module functions properly, but the desired effects of that good reasoning turn out badly, because the actual environment differed in important respects from the environment of evolutionary adaptation.

For instance, a subject doing a deontic version of the Wason selection task correctly interprets the travel rule conditional and proceeds to argue that the p and not-q cards must be turned. Here the subject reasons well because the cheater detection module is triggered properly. Unfortunately, you are fired because, unbeknownst to you, your boss was supposed to increase air pollution (not decrease air pollution) caused by car emissions and enforce a different law: "If you go to Phoenix, you must travel by car." This is because new scientific evidence has proven that air pollution will protect us from aliens that are hovering nearby in Alpha Centauri. Clearly, the gap between the EEA and the AE has resulted in the cheater detection module functioning well in an environment where the original payoff of natural selection from the EEA is no longer in force. The wrong deontic law is represented, and so the cheater detection module malfunctions. Once again, misrepresentation is part of the process that leads to malfunction. Naturally, this example must be fictitious because the cheater detection module in our world remains effective. But the point remains: the gap theory would be able to explain such cases just as it explains the fictitious bacteria and bar magnet version of the Dretske example.

Now one might wonder: are all aspects of the proper or actual domain relevant with respect to the successful functioning of a module? Clearly the answer to this question is "No." All those facts that are causally or logically independent of the proper functioning of a module are held fixed. Call them "nonrelevant facts" or NRF. Everything else is allowed to vary and constitutes the set of relevant facts, or RF, with respect to the successful functioning of a module. On my account:

Module reliability (MR): A module is reliable if and only if it usually produces successful results in the actual domain (AD = <RF1, L1, T1>) and would usually produce successful results in possible domains (PD = <RF1 + ARF, L1, T1 + N>) that are relevantly similar to the actual domain.

The actual domain is constituted by the set of relevant facts, RF1, and the laws of nature, L1, that obtain at time T1. A possible domain is an extension of the actual domain that is physically possible relative to the AD given a passage of time, N, and altered relevant facts (ARF). At a given moment, what is physically possible is purely a function of AD. A "successful result" is one like that which occurred in the proper domain such that the proper function was selected for. "Usually" refers to a frequency account of probability, where the frequency is something like ninety percent. A possible domain is "relevantly similar" to an actual domain just in case they share enough of the relevant facts, RF1, that made the module reliable in its proper domain. What counts as "enough" here is an empirical question that only observation can answer. On this account, the notion of "reliability" is fixed relative to the actual laws of nature that do or would obtain in the actual or possible domains that might evolve. For this reason, proper functions operate relative to some set of relevant facts, "RF1," and laws of nature, "L1," at a time, "T1." Reliability is a relative notion.

An example will help to clarify the account. Humans possess a strong innate tendency to draw away from snakes (Marks 1987). Yet, snakes constitute almost no threat to our existence today. However, for our Pleistocene ancestors, most snakes did represent a serious threat. It is plausible that a snake response module was selected for in the Pleistocene period but that the EEA has changed sufficiently that the AE produces many situations where malfunction occurs. The gap between the EEA and the AE explains the inappropriate responses that occur when we perceive the benign garter snake as a life-threatening predator. In contrast to snakes, the automobile represents, statistically, a far greater threat to our existence, but we blithely drive cars daily through heavy traffic situations. Here is an example where it seems clear that a reliable proper function has gone astray because the environment has changed. The proper domain, within which the snake response module was selected for, has changed such that a once successful proper function is rendered unsuccessful in the actual domain. Notice that reliability is relative to the AE. That is what I mean by saying that reliability is relative to a domain: reliability is tensed and indexed to the actual environment. One can imagine the AE being different if, say, most snakes would continue to represent a life-threatening force. Had that occurred, then the snake response module would continue to be effective today.

It might be thought that my account of module reliability confronts a problem that parallels the generality problem for the reliable process account of justification. The generality problem concerns how to slice process types. If we slice them too narrowly, we will derive types that have just one instance, and so the types will be perfectly reliable or perfectly unreliable. But that does not make sense; types must have more than one instance. On the other hand, if we slice process types too broadly, then we will get types that allow certain beliefs to be justified that clearly should not be so counted. For instance, if we count visual perception as a process type then all beliefs caused by perception will be reliable, for example, beliefs about mountain goats formed at 200 yards will be as justified as similar beliefs formed at 20 yards. Intuitively, this is the wrong result.

The generality problem seems insurmountable for the reliable process account of justification because it is (Conee and Feldman 1998). As long as one is determining what counts as a process type a priori—by appeal to the technique of conceptual analysis—the problem will be irresolvable. My account does not suffer a generality problem since the method used to determine modular reliability does not rely on types being picked out a priori. Instead, module types are discovered empirically. We do not create modules, we discover them. The reliability of such module types is explained by the fact that they were selected for precisely because they were reliable in the EEA. In the EEA, these modules were successful because they were reliable. Hence, we are not in the position of having to create an account of module types that is neither too narrow nor too broad. Natural selection has done the work for us. All we have to do is to discover the modules in question. There just is no generality problem for determining module types.

Another possible worry is that I have provided no account of how misrepresentation might occur in the original environment, that is, the Pleistocene proper domain. It would seem that misrepresentations cannot be explained by the gap between the proper domain and the actual domain because there is no gap; the proper domain is the actual domain. But it would strain credulity to imagine that there were no misrepresentations in the Pleistocene proper domain because our modules were infallible. Were that the case, I would have Dretske's learning period problem transposed from ontogenetic time to phylogenetic time. So, the question remains, how do we explain error in the Pleistocene proper domain? The answer to this problem is, I think, straightforward. There is no domain that is, noncontextually, the proper domain. That is, what counts as the proper domain is relative to the (current) actual domain. Hence, the idea of a proper domain is tensed. So, for instance, the Pleistocene period is a proper domain relative to our (current) actual domain. But, the Pleistocene period was also an actual domain relative to the Miocene proper domain. To think otherwise is to suppose that natural selection first occurred during the Pleistocene period. But that is clearly fallacious. The notion of selection is such that, whatever can be selected for, can be selected of. (For more on this distinction, see section 4.2.) Hence, it is perfectly appropriate that—in different senses—a single environment can be both a proper and an actual domain. For instance, our present environment is, looking backward to an earlier period, the actual domain. But at the same time, looking forward to the future, our present environment is a proper domain if selection occurs in it.

According to Millikan, a problem arises for any account of proper functions that requires that they be reliable. The problem is that proper functions need not be reliable in nature, they just need to be successful at certain important moments. As she notes:

Notice that, on this account, it is not necessary to assume that most representations are true. Many biological devices perform their proper functions not on the average but just often enough. The protective coloring of the juveniles of many animal species, for example, is an adaptation passed on because occasionally it prevents a juvenile from being eaten; though most of the juveniles of these species get eaten anyway. Similarly, it is conceivable that the devices that fix human beliefs fix true ones not on the average, but just often enough. (1993, p. 91)

Millikan notes that beaver slaps indicate danger but, very often, they occur when there is no dangerous predator near by. Apparently, many false positives, that is, beaver slaps where there is no danger, are compatible with selection for, and maintenance of, a mechanism that gives rise to an occasional true positive, that is, a beaver slap that does result from the presence of a dangerous predator. In this case, the beaver that slaps the water is a representation-producer and the other beavers in the pond are representation-consumers. This is unlike the bacteria case where the producer and the consumer are lodged in one organism.

But Millikan's story will not work. The relevant question to ask about beavers is this: in those conditions that are relevantly similar to the context within which the slapping function was selected for, does the beaver slap usually or reliably indicate the presence of danger? The answer is "Yes." Of course, if the beavers are at Marine Land in Niagara Falls then we can expect that they will never output anything but false slaps. Or, in a northern lake where most beaver predators have vanished owing to acid rain, we will expect beaver slaps to constitute an almost uniform class of false positives. But where the actual domain and the proper domain are sufficiently similar, the proper functioning of beaver slaps will be reliable and would be reliable in relevantly similar possible worlds. Millikan cites no evidential support for the idea that beaver slaps typically occur for no reason, that is, no reason relating to reliable danger warnings. Absent evidence, I see no reason to accept her word on this point.

A deeper point is that it is hard to imagine that beaver slaps were selected for in the EEA if they were generally unreliable. Why would such a trait achieve fixation if it were unreliable? Imagine the cost to the species of constantly responding to false warning signals. The time, energy, and resources spent could not begin to justify the occasional avoidance of a predator made possible by such a strategy. It is extremely implausible that such a "boy who cried wolf" strategy would pay in terms of genetic fitness for the beaver population. I do not take this hypothetical argument case to be decisive; but more generally, arguing hypothetically that false positives are more cost-efficient than the truth with respect to maximizing fitness (as Stich does in his 1990 book, *The Fragmentation of Reason*) will not work. My counterexample is intended to show that hypothetical arguments, while suggestive, cut no empirical ice. What is needed are facts about the EEA to establish such claims, not hypothetical arguments. Nevertheless, if one must resolve such disputes by appeal to reason, then I think reason is on the side of truth being more instrumentally useful for the satisfaction of our biological needs and other desires and goals.[9] Of course, I do not mean to suggest that truth is the only desiderata ingredient to fitness. For instance, efficiency and speed are other factors that affect the fitness of an organism. Millikan has another example that makes the same point. Most human sperm cells never perform their function. That is, they fail to inseminate the ovum. But clearly, Millikan argues, the function of the individual sperm cells is to inseminate the ovum. Hence, functions need not be reliable and Dretske is mistaken. Here I think Millikan plays it too fast and loose: the relevant mechanism is not the individual sperm cell but the mechanism that creates the sperm. That device is generally reliable at causing pregnancy. Hence, this example will not work.

The real issue that needs to be addressed with respect to reliability is: which environmental elements, in RF1 and L1, are necessary to reproduce conditions relevantly similar to the EEA such that they allow a proper function to successfully occur in the AE, as it did in the EEA? This, obviously, is a complex problem. And, there is a danger that one may rig the game such that only successful instantiations of a proper function will constitute appropriate examples of relevantly similar conditions for the proper functioning of the adaptation in question. One must be sure not to beg the question. Additionally, there is an epistemic problem in that we may lack the ability to adequately reconstruct the necessary data about the EEA. Where that is the case, we will not be able to tell what would count as "relevantly similar" conditions for the successful instantiation of a particular proper function. Of course, this is not a problem that is unique to the philosopher; it is a standard worry in the empirical sciences and physical anthropology. However, I am happy to confront real scientific problems rather than problems that are the artifacts of philosophical speculation, for example, the notion of a representation-consumer.

3.9   Resolving Quine's and Dretske's Problems

I suggested earlier that solving the disjunction problem would help us to resolve Quine's and Dretske's problems. I want now to cash in that promissory note. On my view, the key to resolving Quine's problem is to notice that adaptive problems set the stage for the development of reliable, proper functions. Malfunctions subsequently represent failures of a proper function to operate in the way the device was selected for. Historically, I think beliefs played a causal role in the instantiation of proper functions. My idea is that beliefs were important for articulating the nature of adaptive problems that our Pleistocene forebears faced. The fact that that object in the distance was a predator that might kill me was an important daily insight for our ancestors. False beliefs about middle-size objects that were near by, I think, were rare among our ancestors. False beliefs about such objects, where these objects were our natural predators, were equally rare. True beliefs had adaptive value.[10] I offer this as an empirical conjecture and one that I have no direct evidence for.

The careful reader may find it ironic that I would appeal to evolutionary intuitions for which I have no empirical evidence since, after all, I have criticized Millikan on just these grounds concerning the notion of a representation-consumer. But I would argue that the existence of language and belief is just a fact. That we need semantics to understand language is obvious. That language requires an evolutionary explanation seems obvious too. We would not find it controversial to suggest that visual perception require an evolutionary explanation, so central is vision to our biological success. On the same grounds, I would argue that language cries out for an evolutionary explanation. If that is true, at least part of the explanation for the importance of language is that language provides a vehicle for truth and truth has instrumental utility for biological and other goals we might have (see chapter 6). Hence, I think my evolutionary claims about true belief have some reasonable chance of being correct, unlike Millikan's evolutionary claims about the existence of representation-consumers. For this reason, I would deny that I have committed the sin that I attribute to Millikan and so also deny that I am being inconsistent here.

That said, I think that, historically, false beliefs sometimes constituted that part of the causal sequence that resulted in the occurrence of malfunctions. Here I am discussing only those cases where beliefs played a causal role and where the nature of the adaptive problem was, in some way, misidentified. To answer Dretske directly, the specificity of a belief can be picked out as a function of the sort of belief that would be appropriate in the context of correctly identifying adaptive problems in the AE. Divergence from the ancestral conditions of the EEA would cause misidentifications in the AE. Where beliefs were important causal players, the results of evolution provide answers as to who had mostly false beliefs and who had mostly true beliefs. Just ask yourself: which species survived?

To answer Quine, the correct interpretation of a foreign speaker's utterance is the one that comes closest to picking out those types of beliefs that successfully played a causal role in identifying adaptive problems, such that the instantiation of the proper function of a module occurred. For the field linguist to interpret the verbal behavior of a native correctly the linguist must understand the adaptive problems that the native's ancestors faced. This will allow us to distinguish between the types of beliefs that would have been crucial for the successful recognition of adaptive problems in the ancestral environment of the native. For our ancestors, identifying natural kinds that were predators would have been more valuable, presumably, than identifying the minute constituent parts of those predators. Belief types that had utility for avoiding our natural predators would be crucial. This much seems straightforward. In effect, true types of beliefs would historically have occurred as a function of their role in the successful instantiation of reliable, proper functions. False types of beliefs would have historically occurred as a function of their role in the unsuccessful instantiation of normally reliable, proper functions.

Of course, I do not mean to suggest that all false beliefs occurred in this way, but part of the origin of error must have occurred along the lines that I have just articulated. Admittedly, the field linguist will not be able to explain all or even most cases of error in this way, nor can this approach pretend to be sufficient for successful radical translation. But, I contend, this strategy may well be useful. I agree with Dretske when he says that "if the mind—or, better, that set of facts that collectively constitutes the mind—is not good for something, and by good for something I mean good for helping one understand why the system possessing it does what it does, then I don't see the point in having a mind. Why bother thinking if the fact that you think, and facts about what you think, do not—sometimes at least—explain why you behave the way you do" (1990, p. 6). My account of false belief or misrepresentation as a causal player in malfunction constitutes half of the story about why meaning mattered historically. The other side of that coin clearly is the role that truth played in the successful instantiation of proper functions.

3.10   Fodorian Objections

Fodor has masterfully detailed the problems that teleological accounts of misrepresentation face in *Psychosemantics* (1987, chapter 4) and in *A Theory of Content and Other Essays* (1990a, Part 1). I want to focus on part 1 of *A Theory of Content*. The central objection that Fodor articulates concerning teleological accounts is, in my view, the fact that such historical accounts, to be successful, need to employ counterfactuals but cannot do so on a Darwinian solution to the disjunction problem. Here is how he puts the point:

Third (and this is the crucial point), going counterfactual to define function (and hence content) would be to give up on a Darwinian solution to the disjunction problem since utility that accrues only in counterfactual environments doesn't produce actual selectional advantages. This means that you can't reconcile appeals to counterfactual advantages with an analysis that construes content and function in terms of selection history. (Fodor 1990a, pp. 75–76)

Fodor cites the case of the brightly colored fish that, according to legend, are found in sunless ocean deeps. It cannot be the case, he urges, that such fish are brightly colored because it would be an advantage for them if their environment were lit up. The properties of potential domains cannot provide reasons for the existence of present traits in the actual domain. He is right about this case, but does it follow that there is no way to build counterfactuals into our account of proper functions? I do not think so.

On my account, the reliability of the proper function of a module supports counterfactuals in the following sense. My definition of the reliability of the proper function of a module builds into it the notion of a possible domain. Such domains constitute counterfactual worlds and the account specifies what reliability would amount to in such worlds. Roughly, on condition that the AD is sufficiently like the PD, the module will be reliable. Where the AD is not sufficiently like the PD, the module will not be reliable in the sense that the proper function will not be successfully instantiated. I make no claim to the effect that the module will be reliable in all possible worlds. The relevant set of counterfactuals that are picked out to elucidate the notion of a reliable, proper function of a module are just those that do and would allow the successful operation of that module in actual and possible domains. In this way, Fodor's central worry about teleological accounts is laid to rest. At the same time, notice that this response handles another worry of Fodor's concerning how to decide which counterfactuals are the ones that count. The counterfactuals that count are just the ones mentioned above.

Fodor has another problem with teleological accounts: he thinks that purveyors of such accounts often commit themselves to the idea that particular beliefs are selected for their causal role in mediating successful behavior in an environment. He made this point in his "Reply to Dretske's 'Does Meaning Matter?'" (1990b) and in part 1 of *A Theory of Content* (1990a). Here is how he puts the point in the latter work:

Millikan thinks that beliefs, desires and the like must have "proper functions," and she thinks this because she thinks that "there must, after all, be a finite number of general principles that govern the activities of our various cognitive-state-making and cognitive-state-using mechanisms and there must be explanations of why these principles have historically worked to aid our survival" (55).

But the assumption that the mechanisms that make/use cognitive states have functions does not entail that cognitive states themselves do. And the assumption that it's useful to have cognitive states themselves does not entail that you can distinguish among cognitive states by reference to their uses. It's a sort of distributive fallacy to argue that, if having beliefs is functional, then there must be something that is the distinguishing function of each belief. The function of the human sperm cell is to fertilize the human ovum; what, then, is the distinguishing function of this sperm cell? (1990a, pp. 65–66)

In the former article, he asserts that Dretske thinks:

"Beliefs function to mediate the integration of an organism's behaviour with its environment," or, as Fred puts it, ". . . cognitive processes are processes whose job it is to coordinate behaviour . . . with the conditions . . . on which satisfaction of needs and desires depend. . . ." This sounds comforting biologically, and if you like the way it sounds, it's ok to say it. But don't then commit the distributive fallacy of supposing that for each belief there exists an environment-behaviour correlation that it is its function to mediate. (Fodor 1990b, p. 34)

Fodor is right. Particular beliefs do not have functions any more than particular sperm cells have functions. That is why, on my account, I have suggested that particular types of beliefs have played a causal role in instantiating proper functions in actual domains because they (historically) helped to identify adaptive problems. On my view, beliefs do not have proper functions. Rather, true beliefs played a causal role in successfully identifying adaptive problems for our forebears. Within Cosmides and Tooby's massive modularity picture of the mind (that I have adopted), only modules can have proper functions. Second, these proper functions are reliable. In short, my account avoids Fodor's distributive fallacy worry, unlike many other teleological accounts of mental content.

Another worry that Fodor develops at length in *A Theory of Content* is that it will always be possible to tell two stories about belief in a Darwinian teleological account. Consider the famous example about the frog's snap-guidance mechanism: it seems possible that the frog is responding to beliefs about flies, that is, fly-beliefs trigger the snap-guidance mechanism. Alternatively, says Fodor, the triggering belief might just as well be about little ambient black things. His claim is that there is no way to cut this disjunctive slack. Evolutionary theory cannot help us solve the disjunction problem. But Fodor is mistaken about this point. There is a world of difference between flies and little black ambient things. Little black ambient things might be poisonous or nonnutritious, while flies are nutritious. Such differences matter a great deal for evolutionary purposes, and that is one reason why they are reflected in the assertive content of our beliefs. In conversation, he has indicated to me that he thinks that the individuation of beliefs via propositional attitudes is so fine grained that, in principle, it is impossible to reconstruct the intensional idiom by appeal to a notion such as "selection for," or any other Darwinian semantical notion. The Darwinian resources available for the explication are too crude for the job. His claim is that belief is hyperintensional: even when p and q are logically equivalent, one can believe p while failing to believe or disbelieving q. So natural selection cannot distinguish between logical equivalents and cannot even distinguish between nomological equivalents.[11]

In fact, Fodor doubts that "selection for" is a viable notion at all because, unlike the extensional notion of "selection" that Darwin provided, Sober's "selection for" is an intensional notion. I think he is wrong to think that Darwinian semantics cannot reconstruct the fine-grained facts about propositional attitudes for the following reason. The notion of an adaptive problem helps to fix the content of beliefs crucial to the successful instantiation of proper functions. Because that is the case, worries about picking out the crucial belief can be quieted. Consider a case that Cosmides and Tooby mention involving the sexual domain. In this domain, error = sex with kin. Mistaking a family member for a nonfamily member in this context can produce genetic disaster. There is no alternative interpretation of the belief that Fodor could cite that would have produced the correct belief when things go well, or the wrong belief, when genetic disaster occurs.

There is no representational slack or disjunctive slack to be found in such cases.

Fodor would argue that there would always be at least two ways to describe this case such that I might think that sex with kin is wrong while approving of sex with a family member and fail to notice that these are nomological equivalents. Natural selection will not be able to distinguish these two beliefs because it works extensionally, but we are capable of believing the first claim while denying the second claim. But is this true? Isn't the assertive content of these two notions identical such that once we have removed all verbal error, no error is possible? That is the view that I think makes sense. If we take the view that mental content should be construed broadly then these two claims are equivalent since their truth conditions are the same. They are extensionally equivalent. Now Fodor favors a narrow-content construal of meaning because he thinks that broad-content individuation will miss generalizations that narrow-content individuation can express (Fodor 1994, p. 34). This simply amounts to reasserting his view that Darwinian semantics cannot pick up on the hyperintensional nature of belief. But, if mental content is given a broad construal, then the stars are in alignment: Darwinian semantics and broad content are given extensional treatments. More generally, to discredit my teleological story, it will not do to point to merely logically possible disjunctive problems. Such fairy-tale ambiguity about belief content will cut no disjunctive ice. The relevant issue is: is it physically likely that disjunctive problems exist where the crucible of evolution, red in tooth and claw, is involved? The answer is "No." Less picturesquely, is there no way to determine which belief would have been essential for the successful instantiation of a proper function? The answer to this question is, clearly, "Yes." It does matter, from the evolutionary standpoint, that it was exactly a kin member that Jones had sex with. There is no room for disjunctive slack where such fundamental issues are at stake. The daydreams of the philosopher just miss the boat in such cases.

At the end of the day, whether Darwinian semantics is successful or not cannot be determined a priori as Fodor would have it. That is, there can be no "in principle" reasons to reject such a project. This is so because the success or failure of Darwinian semantics is an empirical issue, not a conceptual issue. We may, for instance, have difficulty determining what the crucial conditions in the EEA were that led to the selection for a particular property. As such, we may be unsure as to whether a particular error has its roots in an

EEA/AE gap or elsewhere. But such issues are, finally, empirical in nature.[12] As to whether the "selection for" notion is intensional and so whether its use begs the question from the outset, my response is as follows. Sober certainly did not have an intensional sense of "selection for" in mind in his book, *The Nature of Selection* (1984). And I can find no place in the book where he uses the notion in that way. So I see no reason to doubt him on this issue.

3.11   Conclusion

If what I have argued is correct, the disjunction problem can be resolved by appeal to the gap theory as it applies to proper functions. The context within which such proper functions occur is the massively modular conception of the mind recently defended by Cosmides and Tooby. The account does not inflate the representational abilities of such modules, as Dretske would insist, but it does resolve the disjunction problem using the possible domain/actual domain gap approach. It explains what is right about Fodor's asymmetric dependence account while biologizing Fodor's insight using the systematic biological categories that are captured by the proper function/malfunction distinction. In effect, representational error is part of the process that, in a crucial sense, causes malfunction. The account dispenses with the metaphysically otiose notion of a representation-consumer while preserving the core advantages of Millikan's proper function account. Finally, it resolves the problems of Quine and Dretske on the heels of its solution to the disjunction problem. It turns out that meaning matters because truth and falsity matter. In chapter 4, I turn to the other side of the bivalence issue by looking at truth, instead of error.

4 Darwinian Algorithms and Indexical Representation

In this chapter, I want to analyze the sometimes subtle connections between evolution, truth, reliability, and rationality. Contrary to received opinion, I think truth is closely connected to reliable processes by way of evolution. Rationality theory, I will argue, provides the evidence for this assertion. The claim that true belief is a useful commodity should strike no one as perverse. If I am to eat that red berry on that shrub it had better be the case that its consumption will not terminate my life. There may be exceptions to the above claim, cases where "ignorance is bliss" or "a little knowledge is a dangerous thing," but a generally false belief set just cannot, by and large, be an advantage for humans. In fact, I am almost embarrassed to have to defend the claim that false beliefs diminish an organism's inclusive fitness, so entirely preposterous does its negation seem to me. But defend it I will.

4.1 Stich's Argument against Reliable Inferential Systems

Let me first introduce a distinction between false positives and false negatives. To infer p when p is not the case is to utter a false positive. To infer not-p when p is the case is to utter a false negative. Consider the example I began the chapter with. If I have a false negative belief about poisonous red berries, I will not live to write about the experience if I eat such berries. That is, if I believe "that red berry is not poisonous" when it is poisonous then I am a dead duck. If, on the other hand, I endorse the false positive that "that red berry is poisonous" when it is not then I pay no penalty. In *The Fragmentation of Reason* (1990), Stephen Stich used this sort of example to argue that a more reliable inferential system may trail a less reliable one in external fitness. But what is external fitness?

Elliot Sober distinguishes the internal from the external fitness of a genetic program by noting that internal fitness has to do only with the efficiency of the program considered by itself.[1] Comparing a good genetic program with a good computer program, he notes that: "A good program will not only generate the right output for the right input, it will do so economically. It will not use up too much of the computer's memory, nor will it be a drain on the energy source on which the computer runs" (Sober 1981, p. 105). External fitness, in contrast, is such that one genetic program is fitter than another if, ceteris paribus, its input/output pairings are more conducive to survival and successful reproduction (Stich 1990, p. 60).

Stich's claim is that adopting a cautious, risk-aversive inferential strategy that results in mostly false positive beliefs may well tend to produce a higher level of external fitness than adopting a risky inferential strategy that results in mostly false negative beliefs. Hence, the risks attached to adopting a more reliable inferential strategy result in a less externally fit organism. His point is that one false negative, for example, "That red berry is not poisonous," combined with many true negatives may result in a generally reliable inference system. But this system will not be as externally fit as a system with many false positive beliefs, for example, "That red berry is poisonous," and so it may also be a generally unreliable inference system. It follows that it is entirely possible that there has not been selection for reliable inferential systems. Stich concludes that someone who wishes to provide an evolutionary foundation for reliabilism cannot successfully run this line of argumentation.

Let us grant that there may be cases where believing false positives will be more fitness enhancing than believing false negatives. Believing that red berries are poisonous when they are not is less dangerous than believing that red berries are not poisonous when they are, where consumption of such berries follows. Of course, if all one will eat are red berries then one loses either way: one starves or dies from poisoning. The issue is: does Stich's argument show that evolution might not favor reliable inferential systems, as they will be, generally, less externally fit? The answer, I think, is "Yes."

The fact that believing lots of false positives can be safer than believing lots of false negatives makes it entirely possible that some reliable inferential systems will not be favored by natural selection. The interesting question, however, is whether this possibility is likely to obtain. After all, the class of physically possible events is much larger than the class of physically likely events. What we want to know about in asking whether evolution has produced reliable inferential systems is the latter sort of possibility. That is: given everything we know about human cognition, is it physically plausible that evolution has produced reliable inferential systems? The answer to this question I think is "Yes." Of course, Stich's false positive argument cannot establish a negative answer to this question (nor is it intended to). At best, that argument shows that particular false beliefs can be very bad for your health. What it does not show is that, generally, false beliefs will be more externally fitness enhancing than true beliefs.

Stich tries to finesse us when he adds that "a very cautious, risk-aversive inferential strategy—one that leaps to the conclusion that danger is present on very slight evidence—will typically lead to false beliefs more often, and true ones less often, than a less hair-trigger one that waits for more evidence before rendering a judgement. Nonetheless, the unreliable, error-prone risk-aversive strategy may well be favoured by natural selection" (1990, p. 62). Here, as elsewhere in philosophy, the careful selection of examples can make all the difference. Instead of a cautious system that has an excess of false positives, let's consider an incautious system that has an excess of true positives. Consider the case where I quickly form true beliefs about buses in my natural habitat and my friend slowly comes to false conclusions in this regard. I quickly step out of the way of oncoming buses with the aid of a true belief; my friend eventually concludes that the bus he sees is a bus facsimile carefully constructed to make a deep philosophical point by a brilliant, if slightly deranged, philosopher. He holds his ground only to buy the farm. In such a case it would seem that true belief or accurate representation has some purchase on survival and external fitness.[2]

What should be noted in all of this is that conceptual arguments about what is physically possible simpliciter cut very little empirical ice. Stich introduces a red herring by focusing on the wrong question. But I think this tendency is of a piece with the fact that reliabilists have tended to be silent or modest about the evolutionary foundations for their position. The direct evidence for the evolution of cognition is relatively recent and is not generally well known by philosophers.[3] Since this is the case, one hears talk, such as Stich offers, about what "may well" be the case or about what is "entirely possible" as concerns the evolution of cognition in terms of reliable inferential systems. Stich does well to point out that standard evolutionary considerations do not, by any means, make it obvious that reliable inferential systems have been selected for. Nevertheless, there is some compelling empirical evidence from Leda Cosmides that, I think, suggests that at least some reliable inferential systems were selected for.[4]

To help prepare the ground for what I will eventually have to say about the empirical evidence, I want to offer the following argument:

(1) It is physically likely that possessing mostly true beliefs would be an evolutionary advantage.

(2) But evolution cannot select for true belief directly.

(3) Reliable processes could produce mostly true beliefs and such processes could be selected for.

(4) There are no alternative mechanisms that are likely to have produced mostly true beliefs.

Therefore, reliable processes may well have been selected for.

We need not require that I always get the right answer for my point to hold, only that I generally get the right answer. After all, reliabilists have never held that reliable processes are infallible.[5] Such a strong requirement would be implausible. Rather, the idea is that cognitive processes that tend to produce the truth will be selected for. One need not fear, in other words, that evolutionary Panglossianism has been carried to absurdity. The first premise seems noncontroversial in the sense that true beliefs will be instrumentally valuable regardless of our goals (Kornblith 1993). Premise 2 seems accurate because true beliefs cannot be selected for directly as they are not physical candidates for selection (Dretske 1989). Premise 3 is plausible because reliable processes are candidates for selection and they could produce the requisite true beliefs. Premise 4 seems right; it just is not clear what could possibly count as an alternative mechanism that was not a reliable process and yet delivered mostly true beliefs. I conclude that the conclusion is a reasonable one.

4.2   Selection For and Selection Of

One needs to refine the sense in which the term "natural selection" is being used here. Following Stephen J. Gould and Richard Lewontin, Elliot Sober distinguishes between selection of an object and selecting for a property (Gould and Lewontin 1979). As Sober notes: "To say that there is selection for a given property means that having that property causes success in survival and reproduction. But to say that a given sort of object was selected is merely to say that the result of the selection process was to increase the representation of that kind of object" (1984, p. 100). For instance, the selection of the human chin was a by-product of selection for certain jaw structure properties. The human chin is what Sober calls a "free rider" because it was not selected for, but of.[6] As he notes: "'Selection of' pertains to the effects of a selection process, whereas 'selection for' describes its causes" (ibid.). Fred Dretske has recently employed this distinction to suggest that there has been selection for reliable processes but that, indirectly, this has led to the selection of a very special kind of object: true indexical representations. In humans the form that these representations take, according to Dretske, is that of a belief.

Let me illustrate what is meant by a true indexical belief. Suppose that Hannibal Lecter is approaching me with his barbecue apron on and I exclaim: "There's Hannibal the Cannibal now!" Such a proposition provides us with an example of a true indexical belief. It is a belief about the here and now, and it ought to move me to action. Held in the appropriate circumstances, I think such beliefs can be crucial to our survival, and survival is a necessary condition for reproductive success. I agree with Dretske that there has been selection for reliable processes. But I deny that there has been selection of true indexical representations. To see why Dretske cannot be right about true beliefs, we need to return to the example that Sober borrows from Gould and Lewontin to illustrate the selection for/selection of distinction.

The human chin was not selected for. Rather, certain jaw structure properties were selected for because they made possible proper mastication for our ancestors. An inevitable architectural consequence of the selection for these jaw-structure properties was the chin. Objects that are selected of are termed "free riders" because they need not confer any evolutionary benefit in terms of survival and reproduction. The chin falls in this latter category. In such cases, the increasing frequency of such a free rider trait is not tied to some evolutionary advantage that possession of that trait confers. Instead, at the outset these traits enter as a neutral by-product of some other trait that was advantageous. Now let's consider Dretske's claim that reliable processes were selected for, whereas true beliefs were selected of.

If the analogy is to be exact, then the chin is to jaw-structure properties as true beliefs are to reliable processes. That is, both the chin and true beliefs must be free riders that are neutral by-products of another trait that did result in an evolutionary advantage. But Dretske's motivation for suggesting that reliable processes were selected for was that this would provide an indirect way of getting mostly true beliefs. Dretske thinks true beliefs do confer an evolutionary advantage for humans. As he notes: "Getting things right is not just a useful skill. It is a biological imperative" (1989, p. 89). Since indexical representations are not heritable because they are not traits that could be passed on, the only way to select truth is to select for reliability. Reliable processes (such as good reasoning, perceptual capacities, and other sensory modalities), being traits, were selected for because they produce something that confers a tremendous evolutionary advantage: accurate indexical representations. True beliefs are the product of reliable processes, but they cannot have the status of a free rider, such as the chin. Possessing a chin is not a biological imperative; possessing true beliefs is. Possessing a chin is not an evolutionary advantage; possessing true beliefs is. Hence, half of Dretske's analogy breaks down.

Here is what Dretske should have said: the need for true beliefs explains why reliable processes were selected for just as the need for mastication explains why certain jaw structure properties were selected for. True beliefs were not selected of. In fact, true beliefs cannot be selected for or of, because true beliefs are not physical characteristics and only physical characteristics can be selected for or of. For example, the chin was selected of but it might, at some time, be selected for. Suppose that sexual selection results in the favoring of certain chins insofar as the opposite sex is attracted to males possessing such characteristics. One might find that there is an increasing frequency of "Kirk Douglas–style" chins in subsequent generations. The point is that the kind of thing that can be selected of is exactly the sort of thing that might be selected for: physical characteristics. True beliefs are not physical characteristics; they are semantic items. It follows that true beliefs are not the sort of thing that could be selected for or of. Dretske is mistaken. However, in chapter 6 I will argue that property instances of belief, truth, and justification collectively constitute the set of natural kinds that are the phenomena of knowledge. There is a sense, then, in which property instances of innate knowledge have been selected for. But this is compatible with the claim that true belief qua true belief cannot be selected for or of.

But what, one might ask, was selected of in relation to the reliable processes that were selected for? The first thing to note here is that there need be no free riders vis à vis reliable processes. It simply is not the case that for every trait that is selected for there will be some object that is selected of as a free rider. That said, it is plausible to suppose that the ability to enjoy a beautiful sunset or the ability to do modal logic are by-products of, or free riders with respect to, respectively, perception and good reasoning. More precisely, it is the physical characteristics that give rise to these abilities that are selected of and that could, in a different context, be selected for. Elliot Sober has, in fact, suggested that the ability to do calculus and modal logic may be free riders with respect to the more primitive reasoning abilities that they have their foundation in. As Sober insists: "Granted, there was no selection for the ability to do calculus, but that ability could nevertheless emerge via natural selection. Suppose that the ability to do science and mathematics were correlated with certain simpler skills of reasoning and communication that were beneficial in our ancestral past. Then the capacity for more abstract reasoning would have evolved as a free rider" (1984, p. 24). It is clear that humans employ their native abilities in ways in which such abilities were not originally employed. For instance, perception may have been selected for because this trait made possible the pursuit of food, the avoidance of one's predators, and so forth. The fact that we now employ perception to view a splendid sunset confers no evolutionary advantage on us, though it may result in an aesthetic benefit.

4.3   Human Irrationality and the Free Rider Effect

The proposed approach promises to clarify much that has seemed recalcitrant, if not impossible, for cognitive scientists to explain. Consider the cognitive science literature on human rationality. Kahneman and Tversky, Nisbett and Ross, and many others have over the last few decades produced an enormous number of inventive experiments that collectively seem to prove that humans standardly violate a variety of inferential norms.[7] That is, canons of inductive reasoning and deductive reasoning that are sacrosanct among logicians and statisticians are standardly violated by subjects in various experimental setups. I have, in the past, suggested that where modern science, complex social phenomena, and logic meet, one should not be surprised to find that humans make a variety of errors. This is true even though similar errors would not have been made in the specific environments wherein these abilities were selected for (Clarke 1990). But such an explanation, despite its intuitive appeal, must be fleshed out by appealing to evolutionary mechanisms if it is to be taken seriously by psychologists, evolutionary biologists, and naturalistically inclined philosophers. If Sober is right to think that the ability for abstract reasoning required for science and mathematics was a free rider on the more primitive reasoning capacities of our ancestors, then a solution to the human irrationality problem is available to us. We now have a plausible explanation for both the fact that the results of pure research in science often do not matter much for our evolutionary success and for the failure of many experimental subjects to satisfy the standard canons of good reasoning embedded in deductive and inductive logic.

Here is the solution. The fact that reasoning was and is a reliable process in those domains in which it was selected for is consistent with the fact that alternative uses of these same abilities in science and mathematics may result in systematic errors in psychological experiments and false theories in science. The fact that we have difficulty teaching our students modal logic can be explained in the same way. The sort of abstract reasoning involved in science, mathematics, and logic is the result of a free rider effect. But free rider effects confer no evolutionary advantage. It follows that where our original capacities usually resulted in true beliefs, such free rider capacities need not result in true beliefs very often. Certainly, there is no biological imperative for true representations in these domains in contrast to the domains in which our more primitive abilities originally functioned. In our original habitat, true indexical representations were crucial for the survival and reproduction of our genotype. If I am wrong about there being no bus on the road that I am about to step on to, then I die. To the extent that reasoning was involved in the acquisition of such accurate indexical representations, a primitive reasoning capacity that was reliable must have been selected for. But if I go astray in the employment of abstract reasoning abilities in pure science, modern mathematics, or formal logic, I pay no such immediate price. That is not to say that there will be no price to pay, but the price is not likely to be so high as to endanger my life or cripple my capacity for reproductive success.

There is an issue that needs resolution concerning the nature of the fundamental reasoning capacity that was selected for and how it differs from the secondary, free rider usages to which such capacities later gave rise. As a first approximation, a plausible (but false) suggestion is that our underlying psycho-logic involves deductive rules of inference, like modus ponens and modus tollens, and inductive rules of inference, such as the straight rule. The straight rule allows us to determine the probability of an event as a function of its past frequency among a class of events. So, for instance, if you have rolled 11 with two dice on 82 occasions out of 100, then the straight rule tells you that the probability of rolling 11 in the future is 0.82. A deductive rule like constructive dilemma or an inductive rule like the conjunction rule for independent events from classical probability theory are not likely on the list of rules that were the output of our original reasoning capacity. But we have no hard evidence, and there may never be hard evidence, concerning the exact nature of such a primitive reasoning ability. In general, those inference rules that are crucial for the acquisition of accurate indexical representations are likely to constitute the output of such a *primitive* reasoning capacity. Such a capacity may also have included some primitive analogical reasoning ability.[8] (See section 4.5 for more concrete evidence drawn from Cosmides concerning our *present* reasoning capacity.)

4.4 Connecting Selection and Knowledge

But there are other benefits that accrue from the employment of the selection for/selection of distinction in the way that I have suggested. To set the stage for my discussion of such benefits, I will first indicate what I take to be the central shortcomings of Dretske's and Goldman's epistemology. If one takes the standard view that knowledge is justified, true belief, then a typical move is to suggest that the reason we want justified beliefs is that such beliefs have a good chance of being true. In fact, the defining feature of epistemically justified beliefs, as opposed to morally or prudentially justified beliefs, is that such beliefs are likely to be true. If that were not the case, it seems unlikely that anyone would care about having justified beliefs. Goldman's externalist, truth-linked historical reliabilism provides a way of securing such a linkage between justification and truth. Unfortunately, I think the lottery paradox, the generality problem, and the skeptical concerns of Barry Stroud cause severe problems for Goldman's account as will become evident in a few pages.[9] Internalists, on the other hand, have fallen prey to the problem that giving reasons, or being able to give reasons, does not seem necessary for knowledge, if one thinks that, say, young children and dogs know things.[10] Moreover, if doxastic voluntarism is a false doctrine, as many have argued, then the whole internalist framework is in jeopardy (Clarke 1986a). It is unlikely that we choose our beliefs based on good reasons or any occurrent justificational thought at all. Worse yet, internalist justification can never ensure that a connection to truth has been obtained, and so it cannot stop the epistemic regress problem that it was designed to put an end to.

Dretske and, later, Sartwell argued that justification of any kind is not a part of our definition of knowledge. For Sartwell, justification is something acquired in the process that eventually leads to knowledge, but it is not, strictly speaking, a part of the definition of knowledge. Knowledge just is true belief (Sartwell 1992). Dretske, on the other hand, thinks that reliability theories of justification are "implausible" (1989, p. 100). Divorcing justification from knowledge is, I think, a mistake. It is a mistake because it makes mysterious why it is that we should be so concerned to provide reasons and evidence for our beliefs. One answer that issues from Austin and others is that justification has to do with public assertability conditions. But this view is problematic. Is it just to pacify our peers that we strive to defend our assertions? Such a social explanation can only be part of the story. The rest, if I am right, has to do with the need to know. It is instructive, I think, to see how Goldman and Dretske fail in their attempts to provide a complete epistemology. The weaknesses inherent in their accounts, as strong as these accounts are, can be traced back to where they begin their analyses.

Often, Goldman focuses on the concept of "justification" and, only afterward, explicates the concept of "knowledge." The former has some plausibility; the latter cannot succeed owing to the lottery paradox, the generality problem, and so on.[11] First, consider the lottery paradox. Suppose one accepts a purely probabilistic rule of acceptance that says that we may accept something if and only if its probability is greater than 0.99. Henry Kyburg pointed out that such a rule leads to a "lottery paradox": it justifies acceptance of an inconsistent set of beliefs, each saying that a particular participant in a fair lottery will lose (Kyburg 1961). The set is inconsistent since someone has to win, yet one is justified in thinking, of each individual, that he will lose. Goldman's reliable process account of justification stumbles over the lottery paradox, since it requires only that justified beliefs be the result of a process that "tends" to produce the truth, that is, something like 90 percent of the time. But clearly, that will not do for knowledge given the lottery paradox. Of course, this argument presumes that if the reliability of the belief-producing mechanism is 0.9, then the probability that any belief produced by that mechanism is also 0.9 and thus that justification for that belief is something like 0.9. Why, it might be argued, should we suppose that there is any straightforward move from a reliability measure to a probability measure, especially if we are talking about epistemic probability?[12]

Admittedly, there is some sleight-of-hand here, however. There does have to be some connection between the reliability of the belief-producing mechanism and the justifiedness of that mechanism's output beliefs, since, after all, Goldman maintains that a belief is justified if and only if it is caused by a reliable belief-producing mechanism. And, reliable mechanisms are just those that tend to produce the truth. It therefore must be the case that it is the metaphysical reliability of the process that is justification-conferring for output beliefs. That said, there need not be an exact proportional relation between the reliability of the nonepistemic reliability of the belief-producing mechanism and the epistemic probability that a belief possesses as a result of being caused by that mechanism. However that relation is construed, I submit that we will get the result that the belief arrived at will be susceptible to the lottery paradox. This is so since there is a reliable belief-forming mechanism available to S such that S believes by appeal to reason that in a fair lottery the chances that S will lose when she buys a ticket are at least 0.99. Such a belief would clearly be sanctioned for each ticket holder owing to his or her employment of a reliable belief-forming process, say, good reasoning. Yet someone must win. It seems clear that Goldman's account gets the wrong result here.

The generality problem concerns determining the width of process type appealed to. Goldman argues that a belief is justified if and only if it is caused by a reliable process. A reliable process is one that tends to produce the truth. The generality problem can be posed as a dilemma. If we construe process types too narrowly then a reliable process might have just one instance; all true beliefs will be reliably formed and all false beliefs will be unreliably formed. This is the "single case" horn of the dilemma. On the other hand, if we construe process types too widely then the "no distinction" horn of the dilemma must be faced. For instance, visual perception might be thought to be a process type. But beliefs about cows arrived at from ten feet away seem to be far more highly justified than beliefs about cows arrived at from half a mile away. Yet, the reliable process account has no way to mark this important distinction. Goldman and other reliable process theorists seem to have found no way to specify the degree of generality of process types in a principled way (Conee and Feldman 1998). This remains an important, unresolved problem for the reliable process account of justification.

Dretske, conversely, often focuses on the concept of "knowledge" and, afterward, explains away the concept of "justification" as unconnected to knowledge. The former account appears to have a great deal of merit; the latter, much less merit because it is unclear as to why anyone would care about a notion of epistemic justification that is unconnected to truth and knowledge. Justification gets explained away as only having to do with assertability conditions. But, as I mentioned above, the pervasive role of justificatory considerations in all human endeavors is reasonable precisely because we think there is a connection between justification and truth. The scientist who spends volumes of effort gathering evidence for her theory does so with the hope that the way to truth lies in that direction. *Pace* Laudan, Barnes, and Bloor, truth may well be the central epistemic goal of science. Neither Goldman nor Dretske provides an adequate account of justification and an adequate account of knowledge. This is because neither account succeeds in showing the evolutionary connection between justification and truth that leads to knowledge. Dretske denies that justification is related to knowledge in two senses. He thinks reliable process accounts of justified belief are implausible. He also thinks that internalist accounts of justified belief are relevant only when assertability conditions are at stake.

Dretske and I emphasize the indirect role of evolution in producing true belief. But we part company insofar as he fails to allow justified belief simpliciter, construed as the output of a reliable process, its proper and unique role. Simply put: justification is a necessary condition on knowledge. In saying this, I do not mean to be making the question-begging, normative claim that "justification" should be seen as part of any analysis of "S knows that P" (though I accept this point too). Rather, my point is a descriptive one: the folk-epistemic behavior of cognizers reflects a concern for "justification" as it relates to truth, a concern that Dretske fails to adequately explain. As long as we are explaining our human notion of knowledge (what Goldman calls "descriptive scientific epistemology" in "Epistemic Folkways and Scientific Epistemology" [1992]), we must heed the folk. This Dretske fails to do. Dretske's account of knowledge fails to do justice to this fact, as he denies that reliabilist justification plays any role in reliabilist knowledge. The point of searching for beliefs that are justified is made mysterious by Dretske's re-fusal to acknowledge the connection between justification and knowledge as evidenced in cognizer's folk-epistemic behavior. Goldman accepts the evolutionary connection between justification and truth but fails to explain the exact nature of the evolutionary connection that makes this possible, and so he gives us no reason to believe that the processes that he deems re-liable, are reliable.[13] The result is that his account fails to explain how knowledge is possible.

It is here that the selection for/selection of distinction can be of some help. It provides a framework within which we can begin to see how justifi-cation and truth are naturalistically related. Consider visual perception. On my view, it was selected for. Our perceptual abilities constitute a property we possess that causes success in survival and reproduction. Natural selection is not the only cause of evolution in a species. Mutation, migration, and ran-dom genetic drift also are causes of evolution. But natural selection is the dominant causal factor in evolution. Standardly, an increase in gene fre-quency in a population is identified as what constitutes evolution (Sober 1984, p. 29). My claim is that at some remote point in our ancestor's evolu-tion, those with perceptual abilities were selected for. What was it that was so beneficial about perception? No doubt the acquisition of food, awareness of predators, and such were involved. Jerison (1973) has argued that mam-mals developed their large brains in order to handle specific functional de-mands on them as small, marginalized creatures competing in a world of dinosaurs.[14] The first mammals were nocturnal and needed larger brains to transpose olfactory and auditory inputs into spatial patterns that animals active in the day could handle using just vision. Of course, it must be noted that Jerison's view is speculative and has not, to date, been confirmed.

With the development of language and so belief more recently, a unique form of representing the external world became a reality.[15] I take it that be-lief is just one form of representation. The plant that bends toward the sun has its own way of representing the conditions that it responds to. Other forms of representation can be witnessed wherever organisms exist. Accu-rate or near accurate match-ups of propositions and external world situa-tions makes possible the word–world connections necessary to utter true propositions. True propositions were not selected for, but they were an ef-fect of the selection process that begins with selecting for perception, con-strued as a reliable process, and sometimes ends with true propositions. True propositions, therefore, can be seen as an effect of a selection process. This view is also consonant with current views in evolutionary biology concerning the build-up of our native abilities in the following sense: our linguistic capacity emerges long after our perceptual abilities in evolutionary time (Dennett 1992).

The account presented above can also shed light on some thorny old issues. For instance: is knowledge extrinsically valuable and, if so, why? Plato's response in the *Meno* was to say that true belief comes and goes whereas knowledge, made of sturdier metal, endures and so must be properly tethered. There is something right about this response, but if knowledge does endure, one wants to know how that is possible. Here's my answer. Suppose true belief is extrinsically valuable for our survival and, indirectly, for the reproduction of our genes. That is, suppose our first-order inductions tend to come out right most of the time. We believe that X is a threat to us when X is a threat to us. The problem is that we cannot select for true belief directly because selection works on one's genotype. True beliefs, that is, are not heritable. On the other hand, there can be selection for a trait or property. Vision, I think, was selected for. It is our dominant sensory modality for a reason. Vision-based beliefs tend to be reliable indicators of external states of the environment. As Dretske says about someone who, on receiving a gift of a pair of glasses, wants true beliefs about future newspaper headlines: "There is no way to give the person what is wanted, true beliefs about future events, without giving more than what is wanted. Truth, at least the kind of truth now in question, is like that. It is something you can't buy. The only thing for sale is a means, a reliable process, for producing true belief, a means which, when deployed, thereby produces, not merely true belief, but knowledge" (1989, p. 94). Knowledge is extrinsically valuable because it includes true beliefs and true beliefs are extrinsically valuable in the struggle for survival. Our survival makes possible the perpetuation of our genes—which is, after all, the goal of evolution.

If beliefs caused by reliable processes just are the beliefs that tend to be true then we have a clear picture of the value of knowledge. Knowledge is what we get when we aim for true beliefs by employing reliable processes and succeed in our quest. The concern of the folk to have justified beliefs reflects our untutored recognition that we should seek true beliefs and that the best way to ensure this is to employ processes that are believed to be reliable. There may have even been selection for the capacity to seek out beliefs based on believed to be reliable processes or to notice "existing, valid rational connections" as Robert Nozick argued in his book, *The Nature of Rationality* (1993, pp. 108–109). This claim must be seen, however, as a fairly bold and unsubstantiated conjecture at this stage of empirical enquiry. Rather than manmade Kantian categories imposing an interpretation on the external world, the world has shaped our reasoning capacity through natural selection to fit its local requirements (Nozick 1993; Kornblith 1993). Evolutionary theory has turned Kant's Copernican revolution upside down.

4.5   Residual Worries and Darwinian Algorithms

Richard Lewontin comments in his paper entitled "The Evolution of Cognition": "If it were our purpose in this chapter to say what is actually known about the evolution of human cognition, we could stop at the end of this sentence" (1990, p. 229). We have a highly developed mathematical account of evolutionary processes; we know lots about living and fossil primates and about our species' physiology, morphology, psychology, and social organization. But as Lewontin suggests: "we know essentially nothing about the evolution of our cognitive capabilities and there is a strong possibility that we will never know much about it" (ibid.). Despite Lewontin's demurrals, there are good reasons to think that a kind of evolutionary reasoning was selected for. What I mean by "evolutionary reasoning" is that those reliable processes connected with reasoning take the form of Darwinian algorithms: a plethora of specialized, domain-specific inference rules designed to solve recurrent, adaptive problems in the social exchange contexts that our ancestors, that is, the Pleistocene hunter-gatherer, faced. In effect, my claim will be that there are no universally reliable reasoning processes, but only "reliable-in-a-social-exchange-context" inference rules. Let me offer a general a priori argument and some empirical evidence from Leda Cosmides that might help to make this controversial claim plausible. I begin with the general a priori argument.

The A Priori Argument

Suppose one finds it plausible that truth, considered as an indexical representation of our environment, would be useful in our evolutionary quest. Suppose, further, that vision was selected for as a sensory transducer because it can accurately input the relevant data that then must be processed into an output, that is, something with propositional content. It is this content that must accurately represent aspects of the environment if we are to survive and reproduce. But something is missing from this picture. We have failed to say how the input is processed into accurate outputs or true beliefs. My answer is that good reasoning, considered as a reliable process, is essential to this development of inputs. If we cannot reason validly, either consciously or unconsciously, then our inputs will not be transformed into outputs that we can depend on.

What I am arguing is that to the extent that one believes that accurate vision is essential to producing accurate indexical representations of the environment, one has exactly the same reason to believe that good reasoning is essential for the same purpose. Since this is so one will have equal reason to believe that good reasoning was selected for as one has to believe that accurate visual capacities were selected for. In particular, I think that the capacity to reason well, where it matters for our evolutionary success, was selected for. If the norms that we teach our students are different than the norms that constitute the innate capacity that is part of our native architecture and is likely built into our languages, then the difficulties that we have in passing on deductive and inductive norms to our students will be no surprise. This is because there is absolutely *nothing natural about reasoning in conformity with the rules of the propositional calculus or classical probability theory.* That we possess a reasoning capacity seems clear; what is unclear is the exact nature of this capacity. The following empirical data help to shed some light on the nature of our innate reasoning capacity.

The Empirical Argument

A study done by Leda Cosmides provides compelling evidence for the claim that the capacity for reasoning was selected for (Cosmides 1989). Rather than there being a general reasoning capacity or Russellian psycho-logic, we find a Darwinian plethora of reasoning tricks. That is, we find specialized reasoning skills evident in cognitive processes tied to specific social exchange contexts. Instead of a general reasoning capacity, we find a set of reasoning capacities that are content- and context-driven. As Cosmides says: "the innate cognitive architecture of the human mind does not simply consist of a few powerful domain-general mechanisms, as many suppose, but instead contains a large array of special-purpose mechanisms, designed to solve an array of recurrent, highly specialized, adaptive problems (1989, p. 190). Natural selection has shaped how humans reason, she thinks, by "creating specialized, domain-specific cognitive mechanisms 'designed' to solve discrete adaptive problems by activating reasoning procedures appropriate to the domain encountered" (ibid.).

In particular, this means that there are no innate content-independent cognitive processes such as the inference rules of the propositional calculus. Such rules are content independent in the sense that they generate true conclusions from true premises whatever the content of the premises is. What psychologists have found is that reasoning is content dependent in that how humans reason depends on the nature of the subject matter that they are asked to reason about. The evidence is very clear on this point when it comes to the Wason selection task: the content of some rules results in a much higher percentage of logical responses than the content of other rules (Cosmides 1989, p. 191). Figure 4.1 provides a graphic example of this phenomenon.

This Wason selection task illustrates a robust content-effect in the sense that 75 percent of the students chose the correct answer with the more familiar, concrete drinking age law, that is, (b), while only 4 to 25 percent of students provided the correct response with the less familiar, abstract alphanumeric rule, that is, (a). In all cases the correct answer is p and not-q. This is because the material conditional "$p \rightarrow q$" is false, according to the propositional calculus, only when p is true and q is false. Therefore, one must check only those cases that would falsify the conditional: where p is true one must check to see if the conditional is falsified by the presence of a not-q on the other side of the card, and where not-q is true one must check to see if the conditional is falsified by the presence of a p on the other side of the card. Despite the identical logical form of the law and rule, the success rates of students in answering the question about the conditional at issue differed dramatically, establishing robust content effects.

Cosmides thinks such examples show that our innate, adaptive reasoning abilities display different inference rules than those enshrined in the propositional calculus. As she notes:

It is advantageous to reason adaptively, instead of logically, when this allows one to draw conclusions that are likely to be true, but cannot be inferred by strict adherence to the propositional calculus. Adaptive algorithms would be selected to contain expectations about specific domains that have proven reliable over a species' evolutionary history. These expectations would differ from domain to domain. Consequently, if natural selection had shaped how humans reason, reasoning about different domains would be governed by different, content-dependent, cognitive processes. (1989, p. 193)

a. Abstract Problem (AP)

Part of your new clerical job at the local high school is to make sure that student documents have been processed correctly. Your job is to make sure the documents conform to the following alphanumeric rule:

"If a person has a "D" rating, then his documents must be marked code '3'."
(If   P   then   Q   )*

You suspect the secretary you replaced did not categorize the students' documents correctly. The cards below have information about the documents of four people who are enrolled at this high school. Each card represents one person. One side of a card tells a person's letter rating and the other side of the card tells that person's number code.

Indicate only those card(s) you definitely need to turn over to see if the documents of any of these people violate this rule.

D	F	3	7
(P)	(not-P)	(Q)	(not-Q)

b. Drinking Age Problem (DAP; adapted from Griggs & Cox, 1982)

In its crackdown against drunk drivers, Massachusetts law enforcement officials are revoking liquor licenses left and right. You are a bouncer in a Boston bar, and you'll lose your job unless you enforce the following law:

"If a person is drinking beer, then he must be over 20 years old."
(If   P   then   Q   )

The cards below have information about four people sitting at a table in your bar. Each card represents one person. One side of a card tells what a person is drinking and the other side of the card tells that person's age.

Indicate only those card(s) you definitely need to turn over to see if any of these people are breaking the law.

drinking beer	drinking coke	25 years old	16 years old
(P)	(not-P)	(Q)	(not-Q)

*The logical categories (Ps and Qs) marked on the rules and cards are here only for the reader's benefit; they never appear on problems given to subjects.

Figure 4.1

Content effects on the Wason selection task. The logical structures of these two Wason selection tasks are identical: they differ only in propositional content. Regardless of content, the logical solution to both problems is the same: p & not-q. Although only 4, that is, 25 percent of college students choose both these cards for the abstract problem (a), 75 percent do for the drinking-age problem (b)—a familiar "standard social contract."

Cosmides uses evolutionary theory to develop a computational theory of social exchange. Social contract or social exchange theory analyzes adaptive cooperation between two or more individuals for mutual benefit on the assumption that this is an evolutionary problem that is crucial to human adaptation. Since the adaptive inferences of social contract theory sometimes diverge from formal logic results, it is possible to see whether the pattern of reasoning predicted by social contract theory can explain the unexplained content effects that occur in the Wason selection task. The evolutionary story behind social contract theory depends on the fact that our species spent 99 percent of its evolutionary history as Pleistocene hunter-gatherers. The genus *Homo* emerged about 2 million years ago, and agriculture appeared about 10,000 years ago. Since 10,000 years is just a blink of evolutionary time, and not nearly enough to account for much change given the protracted human generation time, it follows that our cognitive mechanisms should be adapted to the hunter-gatherer mode of life (ibid., p. 194). As Cosmides notes: "Pleistocene small-group living and the advantages of cooperation in hunting and gathering afforded many opportunities for individuals to increase their fitness through the exchange of goods, services and privileges over the course of a lifetime" (ibid., p. 196). Cosmides tests social contract theory against associationism-based availability theories of reasoning and Cheng and Holyoak's induction-based pragmatic reasoning theory in light of the content-dependent results on the Wason selection task.

Availability theorists suggest that subjects' varying amounts of experience with the content domains tested, that is, differential experience, explain the unevenness of performance with respect to one and the same argument form. That is, familiarity with the content should produce better conformity with the propositional calculus. This would support the idea that there is a universal content-independent reasoning capacity whose success, in particular cases, can be enhanced or weakened by the specific content plugged into a form of reasoning. But, in fact, what Cosmides found in part 1 of her study was that instantiations of the Wason selection task involving unfamiliar content led to better results than those involving familiar content, contrary to what one would have expected if availability theory were correct.

In Cosmides's first two experiments, subjects received a sealed booklet with instructions on the first page, followed by four Wason selection tasks on each of four pages. Each task was embedded in a brief story and contained either an unfamiliar social contract problem, an unfamiliar descriptive problem, a familiar descriptive problem, or an abstract problem. Experiments 1 and 2 contained an unfamiliar standard social contract, U-STD-SC, but the contract in experiment 1 was an expressed law of a social group, rather than the private exchange rule of experiment 2. The rules used in experiment 2 were: "If you get a tattoo on your face, then I'll give you cassava root," and "If you give me your ostrich eggshell, then I'll give you duiker meat." In these cases, the contract offerer is identified as the potential cheater. The form of the rule is that of a standard social contract: "If you benefit me, then I will pay a cost to you." In the stories, the potential cheater always received his benefit before he had to pay the required cost (ibid., pp. 211–212).

In addition to this Wason selection task, subjects were asked to solve three other Wason selection tasks in experiment 2:

U-D: Unfamiliar descriptive

AP: Abstract problem

F-D: Familiar descriptive

The unfamiliar descriptive rules used in experiment 2 were: "If a man has a tattoo on his face, then he eats cassava root," and "If you have found an ostrich eggshell, then you eat duiker meat." The abstract problem was a non–social contract prescriptive rule; it was included because abstract problems are commonly used as a standard for assessing availability. Cosmides's first experiment involved an unfamiliar social contract that was an expressed law of a social group rather than a private exchange rule. The results are shown in table 4.1. Note that the unfamiliar social contract rule used in both experiments produced results in accord with social contract predictions but inconsistent with what one would expect according to availability theory. That is, the correct answer success rate for experiment 1 was 75 percent and 71 percent for experiment 2. Social contract theorists predict a "high" correct response rate to these rules, whereas availability theorists predict a "low" correct response rate concerning such unfamiliar rules. This shows that it is not unfamiliarity that is the crucial factor concerning content effects on the Wason selection task, but the presence or absence of a social contract rule embedded in the tested material conditional. This result is borne out further with the unfamiliar descriptive problems where no social

Table 4.1

Experiments 1 and 2, predictions and results: percentage of subjects choosing
P & not-Q or not-P & Q for each problem (n = 24)[a]

	P & not-Q responses			
	Predictions		Results	
	Social contrast	Availability	Exp. 1	Exp. 2
U-STD-SC:	High	Low	75	71
U-D:	Low	Low	21	25
AP:	Low	Low	25	29
F-D:	Low	Middling to low	46	38
	not-P & Q responses			
	Predictions		Results	
	Both theories[b]		Exp. 1	Exp. 2
U-STD-SC:	Very low		0	0
U-D:	Very low		0	0
AP:	Very low		0	0
F-D:	Very low		0	0

[a]Table 4.1 compares the results obtained in Experiments 1 and 2 with the predictions
of social contract theory and of availability theory (assuming that responses are determined by either SC algorithms or availability, but not both). In Experiment 1 the
social contract expressed a law, whereas in Experiment 2 it expressed an exchange between two persons, U-STD-SC = unfamiliar standard social contract; U-D = unfamiliar descriptive problem; AP = abstract problem; F-D = familiar descriptive problem.
[b]N.B.: not-P and Q is a very rare response on Wason selection tasks. It involves the failure to choose the P card, which is almost universally chosen, and which even availability theorists concede is guided by at least a rudimentary understanding of logic
(Evans and Lynch, 1973; Pollard, 1979). In addition, when chosen with Q, the sub-
stitution of not-P for P violates ordinary notions of contingency as expressed in En-
glish (why say "If P then Q" when one means "If not-P then Q"?). No availability
theorist has ever predicted this reponse. Both hypotheses predict a *very* low percentage for all problems other than a switched social contract, for which, according to social contract theory alone, it is the predicted response.

contract was involved. Here, social contract theory predicts a low success rate, and this result does obtain: in experiment 1 the rate is 21 percent while in experiment 2 it is 25 percent.

Cheng and Holyoak have tried a strategy similar to that of the availability theorists in the sense that they also posit content-independent cognitive processes to explain human reasoning. But they push the same explanatory variables back one step by suggesting that humans reason using "pragmatic reasoning schemas" that were induced through recurrent experience within goal-defined domains (Cosmides 1989, p. 191). The schemas are content dependent, whereas, the inductive cognitive processes that give rise to such schemas are content independent. Differential experience is a key variable used to explain which schemas are built and which are not. For instance, the following is a permission schema: "Rule 1: If the action is to be taken, then the precondition must be satisfied." Cheng and Holyoak think that most of the thematic problems that subjects have done well on are permission rules, such as rule 1. All social contract rules involve permission, but not all permission rules involve a social contract. This, as Cosmides notes, is because the social contract statement: "If one is to take the benefit, then one must pay the cost," entails the permission rule: "If one is to take action A, then one must satisfy precondition P." But the reverse is not true. All benefits taken are actions taken, but not all actions taken are benefits taken. As Cosmides notes: "A permission rule is also a social contract rule only when the subjects interpret the 'action to be taken' as a rationed benefit, and the 'precondition to be satisfied' as a cost requirement" (ibid., p. 237). This makes the domain of the permission schema larger than that of the social contract algorithms. This difference has empirical consequences. In particular, permission rules that are not social contracts should result in content effects on the Wason selection task; according to social contract theory, this should not happen. In part 2 of her study, Cosmides establishes the falsity of the pragmatic reasoning theory's permission rules in that non–social contract permission rules fail to result in content effects on the Wason selection task.

For instance, in experiment 5 subjects attempted to solve two Wason selection tasks. Each test booklet involved two rules, one occurring with a social contract surrounding story and the other rule occurring with a non–social contract permission rule story. The rules were: "If a student is to be assigned to Grover High School, then that student must live in Grover City,"

Table 4.2

Results

Percentage P & *not-Q* responses:	

Social contract prediction:
Social contract > non-SC permission
  high   low
Exp. 5:   75% > 30%
Exp. 6:   80% > 45%
	Permission schema prediction:
	Social contract = non-SC permission
	  high high

Just as social contract theory predicts, the social contract problems elicited far more P & *not-Q* responses than the non-SC permission rules, which lacked a cost-benefit structure (Exp. 5: 75% vs. 30%: $Z = 2.85$, $p < .0025$, $\phi = .45$. Exp. 6: 80% vs. 45%: $Z = 2.29$, $p < .0115$, $\phi = .36$). This was true even though the non-SC permission rules had a "social purpose". Permission schema theory does not predict, and cannot account for, this result.

and "If a student is to be assigned to Milton High School, then that student must live in the town of Milton." The surrounding story for the social contract problem had it that being assigned to Grover High was a benefit (compared to being assigned to Hanover High), while living in Grover City is a cost (compared to living in Hanover). The surrounding story for the non–social contract permission problem gave the rule a social purpose: following the rule will allow the board of education to develop the statistics needed to assign teachers sensibly to each school. No mention was made of costs or benefits with respect to the rule in this second case; both places and schools are, therefore, portrayed as being of equal value.

Experiment 6 was identical to experiment 5 except that instead of having a culturally familiar setting, such as rules in a local board of education, the rules were set in the fictitious cultures described in experiment 1. The rules were also those mentioned in experiment 1: "If a man eats cassava root, then he must have a tattoo on his face" and "If you eat duiker meat, then you have found an ostrich eggshell." The non–social contract permission problems gave these rules a social purpose, but no costs or benefits were involved (Cosmides 1989, p. 245). The social purpose was one that would benefit the whole community: the purpose was to ration staple foods so as to avoid extinction. Eating one of the staple foods versus the other benefited no individual differently. The results are shown in table 4.2. The results show that the percentage of correct responses where social contract rules were employed was much higher than where non–social contract permission rules were used. For instance, in experiment 5, 75 percent of subjects selected the right answers concerning the social contract rule at issue, while only 30 percent of subjects selected the right answers where a non–social contract permission rule was at issue. This is exactly what one would have predicted if Cosmides's social contract theory were correct and Cheng and Holyoak's pragmatic reasoning schema approach were incorrect. This suggests that the cost–benefit representations of the social contract theory have psychological reality whereas the induction-based pragmatic reasoning permission schemas do not. That was the result of part 2 of Cosmides's study.

To conclude, Cosmides's view is that there has been selection for a large array of special-purpose mechanisms that she calls "Darwinian algorithms." The contrary claim, that the innate cognitive architecture of the brain contains a few powerful domain-general mechanisms, is not supported by Cosmides's data. The long-standing attempt by association-based theorists to explain content effects on the Wason selection task by appeal to availability or familiarity has no empirical support. Hence, the content-independent domain-general mechanisms posited by such theorists fail to possess psychological reality. A similar point holds true for the induction-based pragmatic reasoning theory of Cheng and Holyoak. There is no reason to suppose that there are induction-based cognitive processes that are content-independent. In short, the attempt to explain the content effects on the Wason selection task by appeal to the familiarity of the content, that is, availability theory, or the presence of permission rules, that is, pragmatic reasoning theory, both fail to explain the data. According to Cosmides, the fundamental reason that these alternative accounts fail is that their common assumption—that the same cognitive processes govern reasoning about different domains—is false. As she notes: "The more important the adaptive problem, the more intensely selection should have specialized and improved the performance of the mechanism for solving it (Darwin, 1859/1958; Williams, 1966)" (Cosmides 1989, p. 193). The result is that humans possess special-purpose, domain-specific, mental algorithms that help us solve important and recurrent adaptive problems. Human reasoning does involve reliable processes, but the inference rules in question are reliable only within the context of social exchange conditions, conditions like those that our Pleistocene hunter-gatherer ancestors found themselves in long ago. It would seem that being right is nice, but being right when there are benefits or costs at stake is, as Dretske would have it, "a biological imperative."

4.6   Conclusion

On my view, true beliefs are the output of reliable processes that were selected for during the Pleistocene hunter-gatherer period of our ancestors. Those processes connected with reasoning, as opposed to vision or auditory mechanisms, take the form of Darwinian algorithms. Rather than using content-independent cognitive processes such as the inference rules of the propositional calculus, our ancestors acquired a plethora of specialized, domain-specific Darwinian tricks. These cognitive mechanisms were designed to solve specific, recurrent, adaptive problems. Such problems were made manifest in specific, social exchange contexts. Moreover, the content effects on the Wason selection task can best be explained as being due to social contract permission rules. If all of this is even close to the mark, then we should expect to be able to explain much of the puzzling literature on human rationality by appeal to Darwinian algorithms. Humans reason not logically, but adaptively. Adaptive reasoning in appropriate social contract contexts, it would seem, has been sufficient to get us to the truth most of the time. If I am right, the appeal to evolution unlocks the puzzle about human rationality embedded in the human rationality literature and calls into question Stich's argument against reliable inferential systems in one, clean insight. The correction of Dretske's use of the selection for/selection of distinction produces a more complete picture.

Admittedly, the evidence that I have provided is insufficient to completely support Goldman's reliable process account of justification and knowledge. Much more would have to be done for that job to be complete. For instance, Goldman's account would require that I provide similar empirical evidence concerning visual perception, memory, auditory perception, and so on. However, evolutionary psychologists have worked on many of these problems and the evidence so far is promising. But I cannot recount it here. Suffice it to say that the case is a promising one and that the evidence I have provided gives us some reason to believe that the reliabilist picture may well be the right one. That said, the MMRP picture allows that some reasoning may well be nonmodular. Is such reasoning reliable? I do not think that the verdict is out. Abductive reasoning does seem to play a nontrivial role in our cognitive architecture. Inductive reasoning, as I shall argue in chapter 5, seems reliable if problems are posed in terms of relative frequencies. Hence, even in the nonmodular cases, there is evidence pointing to the reliability of reason for the acquisition of truth. But we are still in the early stages of the pursuit of a complete theory of human reasoning, and so we should exercise some caution. In chapter 5, I will argue that we need a richer conception of epistemic justification as it informs discussion in analytic epistemology and philosophy of science. I attempt to provide just such a picture by showing how two senses of justification are connected to each other and to knowledge. In the process, I show how the evidence from rationality theory can, and does, inform such matters.

5   Rationality and the Meliorative Project

It has been suggested, recently and not so recently, by a number of analytic epistemologists that reliabilist and externalist accounts of justification and knowledge are inadequate responses to the goals of traditional epistemology and other goals of inquiry.[1] These philosophers have followed Lawrence Bonjour in claiming that naturalized epistemologists have "changed the subject" in the sense that they no longer address the important and long-standing questions of traditional epistemology. But many philosophers of science decry reliabilism and externalism because they are connected to traditional, analytic epistemology, an outmoded and utopian form of inquiry. In essence, such philosophers castigate reliabilism for "failing to change the subject."[2] Clearly, both groups of critics cannot be right: either naturalized epistemology has changed the subject, in which case the objections of the philosophers of science are uninformed, or, naturalized epistemology has not changed the subject, in which case some of the analytic epistemologists' complaints are unfounded.

But things are actually worse than I have portrayed them; I think both groups are guilty of conceptual confusions that, once clarified, should allow the naturalization project to stand forth in a rather attractive light. Properly viewed, epistemic naturalism promises rich rewards. After clarifying the differences between meliorative and nonmeliorative justification, I consider the implications of this distinction for the critics of naturalism, that is, both philosophers of science and analytic epistemologists. Later in the chapter, I review some of the more recent literature from empirical psychology on human rationality. This recent literature is decidedly more optimistic than that canvased in chapter 4. I suggest how a naturalized epistemology that takes seriously these recent empirical results, and is informed by the meliorative/nonmeliorative distinction, might be developed. I begin with the distinction.

5.1 Epistemological Issues

Meliorative and Nonmeliorative Notions of Justifiedness

I want to contrast two senses of justifiedness. The first, nonmeliorative, notion is necessary for knowledge; the second, meliorative, notion is not.[3] The first notion concerns already formed beliefs whose status we wish to assess from the third-person perspective. The second notion concerns the provision of advice for cognizers intent on updating their beliefs in a rational fashion with the goal of acquiring justified beliefs. The latter is a first-person perspective on justifiedness. The first notion concerns the status of a product, a belief; the second would provide something like Cartesian rules for the direction of the mind. The first sets out a paradigmatically objective standpoint concerning actual justifiedness; the second is a subjectivist notion that provides advice that makes justifiedness likely, but does not ensure justifiedness.

Let me illustrate the first notion. Suppose that I am at a costume party and Mabel asserts: "Marvin is wearing a blue dress, that devil!" Having just been thinking about nonmeliorative justifiedness, it would be appropriate for me to believe that Mabel is justified in her belief about Marvin if her belief actually was caused by a reliable process and there is no reliable process that Mabel might have used such that its output should have undermined the output of the initial reliable process appealed to. In other words, Goldman's initial account of process reliabilism would sanction Mabel's belief about Marvin since her belief depends on the perception of a middle-sized physical object that is near her, namely, her husband Marvin. We adopt a third-person perspective here and suggest that her belief is justified if the appropriate conditions obtain. If, in addition, the belief is true, we can conclude that Mabel knows that Marvin is wearing a blue dress.

Let's now consider an example of the second notion of justifiedness, the meliorative notion. Suppose that I am an American science advisor to the American crew of the Russian space station, Mir, and I want to make a recommendation to U.S. astronaut, Michael Foale, concerning how he carries out experiments on the Spektr module. I say to Foale: "Always use the straight rule when making inductive inferences about objects on Mars." Here I provide advice designed to help Foale pursue inquiry in a rational fashion with the goal of acquiring justified beliefs. This advice, I submit, constitutes an example of a search for meliorative justifiedness. The sort of justifiedness sought is first-person justifiedness that is likely to obtain, I suggest, if Foale follows it.

My claim with respect to these two notions of justifiedness is that the nonmeliorative notion is necessary for knowledge, whereas the meliorative notion is necessary for the pursuit of inquiry. The latter is developed in the pursuit of an inductive logic or set of inductive inferential principles describing proper scientific method. The reason nonmeliorative justification is intrinsic to knowledge is that knowledge concerns already formed beliefs, and that is what is at issue with nonmeliorative justifiedness. In the context of providing a set of truth conditions for the analysis of "S knows that p," Goldman made the following claim in "A Causal Theory of Knowledge" (1967), over thirty years ago. An account of knowledge should provide truth conditions, not verification conditions, and not the meaning of "S knows that p." The point of an account of knowledge and the requisite account of justifiedness in an account of knowledge is to clarify or make clear the objective conditions governing the proper use of the term "knowledge" and "justification" in ordinary language. In this sense, analytic epistemology constitutes a subcategory of ordinary language philosophy where the contours of our standard use of the relevant concepts is made perspicuous. The goal was not to improve on the standards implicit in the folk use of these terms but to make explicit what was dimly perceived, yet implicit, in our linguistic practices. The point was not to provide verification conditions or to tell us how to pursue inquiry or to tell us when we have obtained beliefs that are, from the first-person, subjective standpoint likely to be justified or instances of knowledge. As Goldman noted: "Truth conditions should not be confused with verification conditions. My analysis of 'S knows p' does not purport to give procedures for finding out whether a person (including oneself) knows a given proposition" (1967, p. 371). All of those projects are worthwhile, but none of them is involved in the nonmeliorative sense of justifiedness requisite for knowledge. Rather, they are concerned with another notion: the meliorative sense of justifiedness.

The nonmeliorative sense of justifiedness has the following attributes. This list should be taken to indicate features that an account of this sort would have and is not meant to constitute such an account:

(A) S is N-M justified in believing that p iff p is:

An already formed belief,

objectively justified,

necessary for knowledge, and

Assessable from the third-person perspective.

My claim is that analytic epistemologists typically pursue accounts of non-meliorative justification, since that is the sense of justifiedness necessary for knowledge. In contrast, philosophers of science typically pursue accounts of meliorative justifiedness, since their main epistemic concern is to describe how cognizers ought to update their beliefs if they want to be rational agents or good scientists, or both. As such, the meliorative sense of justifiedness is such that:

(B) S would be M-justified in believing that p iff

p would be subjectively justified;

p would not be necessary for knowledge, but would satisfy doxastic-decision procedures that describe advice for cognizers intent on updating beliefs in a rational fashion with the goal of acquiring justified beliefs; and

p would be assessable from the first-person perspective.

The core contrast is that between already formed beliefs that are objectively justified and yet to be formed beliefs that are subjectively arrived at by following a set of procedures akin to an algorithm. The goal of the meliorative project is to provide advice to cognizers intent on rationally updating their beliefs such that they would arrive at melioratively justified beliefs. The sense of "subjective" in subjective justification that is requisite for meliorative justification is not that anything goes; far from it. Rather, the idea is that to be justified in holding a belief, one must be able to tell from the first-person perspective that one has satisfied a set of epistemic constraints. Moreover, one uses the algorithm to arrive at one's beliefs. Justification is transparent to the cognizer. In contrast, objective justification is not transparent to the cognizer, but it is such that the cognizer is actually hooked up to the world in a metaphysically appropriate way. That is, the cognizer is hooked up to the world in a way that is likely to, though it need not, result in knowledge. Once we make the meliorative/nonmeliorative distinction, the mistakes of the recent literature become clear.

Where Philosophers of Science Have Gone Astray

In my view, when philosophers of science are worried about epistemic justification, they are paradigmatically concerned with the meliorative project. Carnap's interest in developing an objectivist, inductive logic is an exemplar of this sort of project.[4] But, whatever else it was, Carnap's project was not a nonmeliorative account of justifiedness, and, as such, it could not have figured in an account of knowledge. The idea was to provide epistemic advice for an ideal rational agent concerned to update her beliefs in light of incoming evidence. Carnap, no doubt, hoped that the result of following such advice would be the acquisition of knowledge. But, Carnap's inductive logic was not intended as an analysis of "S knows that p," nor was it intended as an account of the nonmeliorative justifiedness requisite for knowledge.

It is important to see, however, that these two projects are connected. Having a sense of what one is pursuing, that is, nonmeliorative justification, even if one admits that all one can be sure of is that one has satisfied meliorative constraints on justifiedness, is crucial. It is akin to the distinction between knowing that and knowing how. For instance, I must first understand what it means to hit the golf ball 350 yards by, say, watching Tiger Woods, before I can begin to acquire the know-how necessary to achieve this goal. Knowing the nature of the goal of inquiry may well be helpful in formulating principles designed to acquire such states. Both notions of justifiedness involve the explication of normative notions in nonnormative terms, and both answers ought to be informed, on my view, by both conceptual and empirical considerations. That empirical psychology and evolutionary theory ought to inform our analysis of meliorative justifiedness is a nontrivial claim. Carnap, for instance, would not have thought that such an appeal was necessary. And even contemporary philosophers of science, who work on inductive inference, rarely appeal to such considerations.[5] At any rate, the pursuit of the meliorative question is made easier by having first answered the nonmeliorative question concerning the proper form of an account of justification and knowledge. As such, these are separate but related problems.

To return to our original objection by the philosophers of science, have reliabilists and externalists gone astray by "not changing the subject"? That is, is the traditional project of providing an a priori, conceptual analysis of knowledge and a nonmeliorative account of justifiedness bankrupt, utopian, and impossible? Is first philosophy a dismal failure, made impossible by accepting the skeptic's unreasonable standards and then, foolishly, trying to meet them? And, finally, do reliabilists and externalists seal their own fate as irrelevant by persisting in the old, wheel-spinning scholastic projects? If I am right, most reliabilists have not changed the subject; the philosophers of science are right about that. Goldman, for instance, persists in thinking that conceptual analysis has a role to play in the provision of an account of what I have called "nonmeliorative justifiedness." Kornblith, in contrast, would have us give up the "concept" of knowledge and justification and a priori conceptual analysis in favor of understanding the actual phenomena at hand.[6] Just as understanding the nature of aluminium is an empirical pursuit, Kornblith argues, understanding justification and knowledge requires empirical, not conceptual, inquiry. Kornblith's conception of inquiry, however, is novel and not the standard, naturalized approach. Conceptual analysis, in Goldman's hands, is such that one must begin from where our folk epistemic notions find us and proceed to provide a scientific epistemology. The first form of inquiry makes no attempt to improve on our ordinary standards, but uses results from cognitive science to clarify our implicit standards.

The second form of inquiry attempts to improve on the folk standards by once again exploiting the results of cognitive science to suggest ways that we can improve our belief-acquisition procedures. This latter project, in reality, is the meliorative one. Implicit in the transition from folk epistemology to scientific epistemology is the use of the nonmeliorative notion of justifiedness to construct a notion of meliorative justification. It is not clear that Goldman sees that this is what is at stake. At any rate, the right response to the philosophers of science is to say that answering the meliorative question requires that we answer the nonmeliorative questions about justification and knowledge first. As such, empirical discovery and conceptual clarification concerning nonmeliorative notions is necessary before we can answer the meliorative question. A naturalized epistemology that is sensitive to conceptual matters is, in this sense, necessary and important for the philosophy of science. An important illustration of this insight has, I think, recently come to light in the context of naturalized philosophy of science.

Harvey Siegel, in a series of insightful papers, has argued that naturalized philosophers of science cannot do without an a priori, conceptual inquiry into the nature of what he calls "categorical rationality."[7] In particular, he has suggested that instrumental rationality presupposes categorical rationality. In contrast, naturalized philosophers of science, like Larry Laudan and Ronald Giere, have argued that only an instrumental notion of rationality is necessary for inquiry, and so they deny the very existence of categorical rationality.[8] But what, for Siegel, is categorical rationality? Categorical rationality involves a priori reasoning in order to give an account of what "good reasons" are where one wants to provide an explication of the epistemic relation that obtains between claim, that is, theory, and evidence. Instrumental rationality, on the other hand, involves a posteriori reasoning in the explication of the causal relation that obtains between means and ends (or goals). For instance, one might use the double-blind methodology as a means to test a drug, where one's end or goal is to determine the medicinal value of a particular drug. Siegel calls such instrumental means–end relations "claims." Schematically:

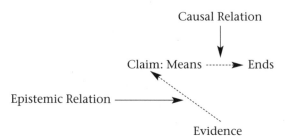

Causal Relation

Claim: Means ------> Ends

Epistemic Relation ------->

Evidence

Siegel's point, in a nutshell, is that the instrumental rationality relation or causal relation that obtains between means and ends in a claim receives epistemic support from the evidence if and only if one tacitly presupposes a categorical rationality concept that explicates the epistemic relation between claim and evidence.

Laudan (1987, 1990) and Giere (1985), in contrast, deny that rationality involves anything more than an instrumental or causal relation. Hence, the relation between claim and evidence must, itself, be a causal one. But this is odd. How could the evidential relation or the support relation fail to be an epistemic, noncausal, categorical notion? Siegel does not tell us much about what categorical rationality as good reasons comes to, but Carnap would have taken the evidential relation to be one that could be explicated by his inductive logic. That Carnapian account is, on my view, one among many possible answers to the meliorative question: a confirmation theory. In my view, Siegel is right to think that rationality is bipartite—instrumental and categorical—and that instrumental rationality (causal rationality) presupposes categorical rationality (epistemic rationality). In my view, there are two kinds of categorical rationality (epistemic rationality): meliorative (first-person) and nonmeliorative (third-person) rationality. These kinds of rationality often result in, respectively, meliorative (first-person) and nonmeliorative (third-person) justification. Moreover, accounts of meliorative justifiedness should be informed by accounts of nonmeliorative justifiedness.

Another way to make this point is to say that an account of first-person, subjective justifiedness (meliorative justification) presupposes an account of third-person, objective justifiedness (nonmeliorative justification). In effect, we use an account of subjective justifiedness as a means to the goal of objective justifiedness. If all goes well, and the objectively justified beliefs are true, then we will know things. But we can never know that our beliefs are objectively justified or that they are cases of knowledge. Fortunately, we can know that p without knowing that we know that p. Carnap's mistake was to think that one could provide objectivist constraints on a notion that had to be, finally, subjectivist in nature: meliorative justifiedness. This point has not been lost on the personalist or Bayesian tradition and, in fact, is signaled by their use of "priors," subjective prior probability estimates.[9] Rules for the direction of the mind can only be rules that we think are likely to lead to the truth. Following such rules cannot guarantee that we will acquire the truth. There can be no Carnapian objectivist measures in our world.

I now turn to the analytic epistemologist's arguments. If what I have argued is correct, then instrumental rationality (IR) presupposes categorical rationality (CR). Categorical rationality is composed of meliorative (MR) and nonmeliorative rationality (NR) and their correlates: meliorative (MJ) and nonmeliorative (NJ) justification. Finally, meliorative justification presupposes nonmeliorative justification. There is a path, then, from NJ to MJ and from MJ to IR. That path, in my view, provides a reconstruction of the foundations of our knowledge of the external world and, in doing so, articulates an ideal method for the acquisition of that knowledge.

So, for instance, suppose that IR is such that one makes the following claim:

(A)   If you use the double-blind methodology then you will be able to determine the medicinal value of drug D.

Here the end or goal is to determine the medicinal value of D and the means requires that one use the double-blind testing methodology. MJ, in this case, would involve the epistemic relation between (A) and the evidence E. Carnap's inductive logic might be used to clarify this categorical rationality relation between (A) and E. As such, it would then tell us how to determine how much epistemic support the claim has relative to the evidence. What Carnap does not provide is an account of nonmeliorative justification that would ground his inductive logic or meliorative project. But suppose that Goldman's initial reliable process account of justification was employed for this purpose. On Goldman's account, S is justified in her belief that p if and only if (approximately) S's belief that p is caused by a reliable process and there is no other reliable process such that it would, were it employed, undermine S's belief that p. This account of nonmeliorative justification could be used to underwrite Carnap's meliorative account of justification, that is, inductive logic, in the sense that Carnap's inductive logic may be seen as constituting a type of reliable process, namely, good reasoning.

The result is that we now have before us part of a reconstruction of the foundations of our knowledge of the external world. If it were a successful reconstruction then it would provide part of an account of an ideal method for acquiring such knowledge. It is an example, though simplified and idealized, of the path from NJ to MJ and from MJ to IR. The example is, of course, not the account that I endorse, but it is meant to illustrate the overall picture, in simplified form, that I have in mind. My hope is that it will clarify matters sufficiently for the reader to see the need for, and crucial role of, an account that connects nonmeliorative and meliorative justification in our pursuit of knowledge. Call such an account a *metaepistemics* in that it parallels the role of metaethics in ethical theory. For the naturalist, such an account would, in effect, link analytic epistemology and philosophy of science by showing how, for instance, naturalization projects in each domain are connected. Metaepistemics as here conceived would also include an account of nonmeliorative justification and knowledge as developed in its conception of categorical rationality. Any adequate epistemology must, in my view, provide such a metaepistemic account in order to ground its "normative epistemic" account of the meliorative project as clarified in its meliorative account of justification. Subsequently, the account of instrumental rationality entailed by one's meta- and normative epistemic theory would fall out as "applied epistemics." A complete epistemological theory would thus be tripartite: consisting of meta-, normative and an applied epistemic account of its subject matter.

Where the Analytic Epistemologists Have Gone Astray

Barry Stroud, Richard Fumerton, and Mark Kaplan have all questioned the approach of externalist, naturalistic, process reliabilism. Stroud questions reliabilism because he thinks that no such externalist stance can possibly answer the Cartesian philosophical skeptic. Fumerton, an internalist foundationalist, thinks reliabilists fail to address the important traditional questions of epistemology. And, Kaplan, a naturalist himself, thinks that process reliabilism fails because externalist answers fail to address the meliorative justifiedness issue, and that is the notion of justifiedness requisite for knowledge. I think a proper understanding of the meliorative/nonmeliorative distinction and its consequences can overcome the problems these authors see with externalism and reliabilism. I begin with Kaplan.

Kaplan   Kaplan rejects the nonmeliorative conception of justifiedness. That nonmeliorative notion represents epistemology on holiday or epistemology denatured, in the sense that an account of justifiedness that does not tell us how to proceed with inquiry, is epistemically inert and, so, unhelpful. As he notes: "The problem is that, if it is characteristic of the nonregulative use of 'justified' that it has no methodological import—that there is nothing in the set of rules to be consciously adopted by an inquirer that calls for her to determine whether any of her beliefs is justified in the nonregulative use of that term—then it is hard to see what point there could be to a system of evaluation dedicated to saying when it is that a person's belief is justified in the nonregulative sense" (Kaplan 1994, p. 353).

What Kaplan, drawing on Goldman, means by "nonregulative justification" corresponds—more or less—with what I have called "nonmeliorative justifiedness," and what he calls "regulative justifiedness" is what I call "meliorative justifiedness." Now Kaplan is happy to naturalize the traditional quest for meliorative justifiedness in the sense that he thinks we ought to use the results of cognitive science to clarify the "biases, tendencies, strengths and weaknesses" of our methodological advice for those seeking truth. Kaplan is committed, therefore, to deploying the traditional approach to methodology in order to develop a theory of cogent argumentation. What I want to suggest is that Kaplan is mistaken to think that the nonmeliorative notion is of no use for this purpose. A well-formed account of nonmeliorative justifiedness provides an objective account of justifiedness that tells us what properties all justified beliefs share, and constitutes one among (at least) three truth conditions on knowledge. By analogy, suppose that it would "make my day" to get from San Francisco to Carmel to eat at Clint Eastwood's restaurant, but that I have no idea where Carmel is. How could it fail to be useful to see, on a map, that Carmel is just below Pebble Beach on Highway 1? An account of nonmeliorative justifiedness serves a similar role vis à vis the pursuit of an account of meliorative justifiedness. It provides an objective account of justifiedness toward which we can point our subjective account of justifiedness. The former is a goal toward which the latter is the means.

Fumerton   Richard Fumerton, likewise, finds the externalist approach problematic, but not because he rejects the nonmeliorative notion of justifiedness. It should also be noted that he, unlike Kaplan, sees no serious role for a naturalized epistemology to play. Fumerton thinks that science cannot help us with our philosophical problems. A proper account in normative epistemology ought to help us answer the skeptic, and it ought to tell us which of our beliefs are justified and why the skeptic is wrong to think that we know nothing about the external world. As Fumerton notes: "Metaepistemological questions concern the philosophical analysis of fundamental epistemic concepts. Normative epistemological questions ask to what the epistemic concepts apply" (1994, p. 324). Naturalism is a metaepistemological position in that it offers conditions governing fundamental epistemic concepts like justification and knowledge. But naturalism itself is inert with respect to answering normative epistemic questions because it leaves that task to neuroscience or other cognitive sciences. That is, a process reliabilist, like Goldman, tells us what all justified beliefs have in common: reliable processes cause them all. But determining which processes in the world actually are reliable is a task for the cognitive scientist to answer, given Goldman's weak replacement division of labor between philosophers and scientists.

For Fumerton, this result renders process reliabilism and, actually, all naturalistic metaepistemological positions inert with respect to telling us which of our beliefs are justified. As Fumerton notes, the skeptic might ask:

"But how exactly would one justify one's belief that, say, perception or memory are reliable processes? The rather startling and, I think disconcerting, answer is that if reliabilism, for example, is true, and if perception happens to be reliable, we could perceive various facts about our sense organs and the way in which they respond to the external world" (1994, pp. 336–337). And further: "None of this, of course, will make the skeptic happy. You cannot use perception to justify the reliability of perception! You cannot use memory to justify the reliability of memory! You cannot use induction to justify the reliability of induction! Such attempts to respond to the skeptic's concerns involve blatant, indeed pathetic, circularity" (ibid., p. 338). Call Fumerton's argument the *circularity argument*. Fumerton concludes that the circularity argument constitutes a powerful reason to reject naturalistic epistemology. Is he right to urge this result? No, and here's why. The problem he wants addressed is the meliorative question about how to update our beliefs rationally so as to acquire justified beliefs. The mistake is to think that an account of meliorative justifiedness is requisite for knowledge or constitutes an alternative answer to the metaepistemological issues that the naturalist addresses. If Fumerton is right to think that naturalism is an answer to the metaepistemological question concerning the analysis of nonmeliorative justifiedness from the third-person perspective, then it follows, by his own lights, that the meliorative question addresses an issue in normative epistemology concerning the epistemic status of beliefs from the first-person perspective. As such, the skeptic's question is couched at the normative level and must be addressed from that level of analysis.

The good news is that answering the metaepistemological question first is logically necessary before one can hope to answer the normative epistemic question. This point holds true as much in epistemology as it does in ethics. After all, suppose that one is an intuitionist at the metaethical level. That stance dictates how to determine which actions are good at the normative level of assessment. It follows that normative ethical judgments presuppose answers to metaethical questions. By parity of reasoning, normative epistemic judgments presuppose answers to metaepistemological questions. And, in naturalized philosophy of science, instrumental rationality presupposes categorical rationality, that is, the meliorative and nonmeliorative projects (and where the meliorative project presupposes the nonmeliorative project), for much the same reason: foundations must be arrived at prior to the application of those foundations.

Stroud   Stroud offers the circularity argument against an "enlightened" or "externalist," but essentially Cartesian, theory of knowledge in order to argue against all externalist theories of knowledge. First, the original Cartesian argument. Much of the *Meditations* is devoted to overcoming the skeptical scenario set out in the First Meditation, where—in essence—Descartes argues that in order to know that p, one has to rule out the logical possibility that one is mistaken, for example, because one is dreaming or being fooled by the evil demon, in believing that p. Descartes's infamous response is to argue that God exists and is no deceiver and that everything in us, such as our capacity to perceive and think, comes from God. Hence, since whatever we clearly and distinctly perceive to be true is true providing that we are careful and trust God's goodness, it follows that we can know much of what we ordinarily take ourselves to know. The enlightened or externalist Cartesian argument against the skeptic would insist that the cognizer does not have to know the truth of the theory that explains his knowledge in order to have that knowledge. All of the other facts about the original Cartesian argument remain the same. As Stroud remarks: "What would be wrong with accepting such an 'enlightened' theory? If we are willing to accept the kind of theory that says that knowing that p is having acquired the true belief that p by some reliable belief-forming mechanism, why would we not be equally or even more willing to accept a theory that says that knowing that p is having acquired the true belief that p by clearly and distinctly perceiving it—a method of belief formation that is reliable because God guarantees that whatever is clearly and distinctly perceived is true?" (1989, p. 43). Beyond the dubiousness of God's existence and, ipso facto, his guarantees, the problem is that we need some reason to think that the enlightened Cartesian story is true. More generally, we need some reason to think that an account of knowledge is true if we are to accept it. According to Stroud, one cannot just appeal to the theory without some independent reason to think that the theory is true on pain of circularity. It will not do to say that if we employ reliable processes and our scientific account of these is true that we will know many things, Stroud thinks, because the externalist, whether of the enlightened Cartesian or process reliabilist sort, is guilty of circular reasoning. That circularity dooms such accounts. In short, Stroud offers the same circularity argument that Fumerton does.

It follows that if my response to Fumerton is successful then the same response applies to Stroud. Both philosophers are concerned with the first-person perspective of someone who is responding to the meliorative question of which beliefs to accept. Since this question is posed from the standpoint of normative epistemology where the skeptic asks her question it only makes sense that process reliabilism, a metaepistemological naturalist position that constitutes a nonmeliorative account of justifiedness, would be an inadequate response. Process reliabilism is an answer to a different, though traditional, question. There are at least two kinds of traditional questions in epistemology: the nonmeliorative and the meliorative question. Process reliabilists have not changed the subject; they answer a traditional question in a perfectly reasonable way—just as Descartes did. Both responses are unsatisfying only if one is confused about the question under scrutiny. Once we get clear that the issue is the nonmeliorative sense of justifiedness, it turns out that the process reliabilist offers an attractive answer to an enduring problem.

Conclusion   One might think, as Kaplan does, that if what I have said about process reliabilism is correct then we can safely ignore it because it answers a question that we need not take too seriously—the nonmeliorative question. But this response, as I have suggested, is a mistake. Kaplan is right to think that the meliorative issue is central: knowing how to proceed with inquiry in pursuit of knowledge is of the first importance. Kaplan's mistake is to think that answering the meliorative question can be done without answering the nonmeliorative question. It cannot. One must know where one is going before one can take steps to arrive there. I turn now to the literature on human rationality to assess the implications of that literature for the meliorative project.

5.2   Human Rationality

Empirical Studies of Inferential Errors

Our perceptual experience of the external world is seamless, integrated, and continuous. But science tells us that our subjective experience is incompatible with the objective facts: We fill in the blanks to get continuity and compensate for the breaks in a variety of ways. Rationality is similar to perception in that it seems unified; it is just as though there is an underlying Russellian psycho-logic that guides thought and language. It often seems to us, as van Fraassen once said (in conversation), that the sentential calculus

Table 5.1

Linda is 31 years old, single, outspoken and very bright. She majored in philosophy. As a student she was deeply concerned with issues of discrimination and social justice, and also participated in antinuclear demonstrations.

Please rank the following statements by their probability, using 1 for the most probable and 8 for the least probable.

(i) Linda is a teacher in an elementary school.
(ii) Linda works in a bookstore and takes Yoga classes.
(iii) Linda is active in the feminist movement.
(iv) Linda is a psychiatric social worker.
(v) Linda is a member of the League of Women Voters.
(vi) Linda is a bank teller.
(vii) Linda is an insurance salesperson.
(viii) Linda is a bank teller and is active in the feminist movement.

underlies our linguistic practices—eleven rules and a bit of luck. Empirical psychology, however, over the last thirty years has sullied this human self-portrait. We make inductive and deductive errors that are widespread and pervasive, and there are content effects on the Wason selection task. Despite attempts to explain away these data by philosophers, I doubt that this can be done. By rigorous logical standards, humans turn out to be irrational in the sense that there are no truth-preserving, content-neutral, domain-general logical systems that humans employ in day-to-day reasoning. More recent studies have tempered the initially bleak picture of human reasoning that emerged in the 1970s and 1980s. Cosmides and Tooby have argued that intuitive inductive reasoning seems better than was suspected. But the overall judgement concerning our intuitive deductive reasoning remains negative.

It has become evident that the inconsistency of human inferential reasoning capacities is the result, in part, of the mind being massively modular. This recognition has had dramatic effects on our accounts of perception, reasoning, linguistic competence, and a host of other issues. The view that I want to recommend is that what I call a *realist, mental adapticism* can explain and bring order to the results on human rationality. Moreover, mental adapticism ought to be employed, along with our best accounts of nonmeliorative justifiedness, to construct accounts of meliorative justifiedness. But, first, we need to clarify some of the empirical literature. There is evidence that we commit the conjunction fallacy and are guilty of base-rate neglect and overconfidence. Consider the Linda case concerning the conjunction fallacy (table 5.1).

In this experiment, 89 percent of subjects ranked (viii) as more likely than (vi). These results are easily replicated. Concerned that subjects might tacitly presuppose that (vi) meant

Linda is a bank teller and is not active in the feminist movement,

Tversky and Kahneman replaced (vi) with

(vi′)   Linda is a bank teller whether or not she is active in the feminist movement

and tried the new material on a second group of subjects (Stich 1990, p. 6). The results were similar. Thinking that the subjects were distracted by the other options, 142 subjects were given the original problem with only (vi) and (viii) and asked which alternative was more likely. Amazingly, 85 percent found the conjunction more likely than the conjunct. According to classical probability theory, the likelihood of a compound event or state of affairs has to be less than or equal to the likelihood of its components, that is, $\Pr(p\&q) = \Pr(p) \times \Pr(q)$, where the events are independent. A number of experiments, like the one mentioned above, seem to demonstrate that people regularly violate this tenet of probabilistic reasoning in the sense that they believe the probability of a conjunction to be greater than the probability of either of its conjuncts.

Moreover, studies with the Wason selection task show that the extent to which our reasoning conforms to the propositional calculus is a direct function of the subject matter we address. That is, there are content effects evidenced on such tasks in the sense that two rules with the same logical form but different content will elicit substantially different results. The abstract versus drinking age example discussed in section 4.5 is one such clear example of this effect. But the very idea of a logic requires a truth-preserving, content-neutral set of syntactic transformations over vacuous place holders such as p, q, and so forth. For this reason, if these data were definitive of our human reasoning capacity it would follow that that capacity does not embody a logic on any standard account of what counts as a logic. If this is correct then the twentieth-century dream of providing a mental logicism, total or partial, is a nonstarter. As long as there are content effects on the Wason selection task, it would seem to follow that we do not consistently obey fundamental rules of the propositional calculus insofar as we cannot handle the material conditional properly.

Initially, Wason and other associationism-based availability theorists inferred that familiarity with the data, that is, differential experience, could explain the content effects on the Wason selection task. The idea was that we did possess a domain-general, content-independent reasoning capacity but that this capacity could be enhanced depending on the familiarity of the content plugged into the system. Later, Cheng and Holyoak argued for an induction-based pragmatic reasoning theory that, like availability theory, posited a domain-general, content-independent reasoning capacity. But they pushed the same explanatory variable back one step by suggesting that humans reason using "pragmatic reasoning schemas" that were induced through recurrent experience within goal-defined domains. The schemas are content dependent, whereas the inductive cognitive processes that give rise to the schemas are content independent. On this view, differential experience is used as a key determinate of which schemas are built and which are not built.

Leda Cosmides, in a brilliant set of experiments, established that neither the associationist-based availability theory nor the induction-based pragmatic reasoning theory can explain the content effects on the Wason selection task. Instead, Cosmides argued that whether or not a social contract is embedded in the Wason selection task rule determines the content effects. That is, if there is a social contract involved, even one not familiar to the subjects, they will do much better on the task—contra the availability theorists. The form of a social contract statement in general is: "If one is to take the benefit, then one must pay the cost." This statement will entail permission rules such as: "If one is to take action *A*, then one must satisfy precondition *P*." But the reverse is not true. All benefits taken are actions taken, but not all actions taken are benefits taken. As Cosmides notes: "A permission rule is also a social contract rule only when the subjects interpret the 'action to be taken' as a rationed benefit, and the 'precondition to be satisfied' as a cost requirement" (Cosmides 1989, p. 237). This makes the domain of the permission schema larger than that of the social contract algorithms. This difference results in empirical consequences. In particular, permission rules that are not social contracts should result in content effects on the Wason selection task; according to social contract theory, this should not happen. It turned out that Cosmides was right: non–social contract permission rules failed to result in content effects. In the early 1990s, Gigerenzer and Hug

Table 5.2
Single-event and frequency versions of Fieldler's (1988) conjunction problems

Single-event version	Frequency version
Linda is 31 years old, single, outspoken and very bright. She majored in philosophy. As a student, she was deeply concerned with issues of discrimination and social justice, and also participated in anti-nuclear demonstrations.	Linda is 31 years old, single, outspoken and very bright. She majored in philosophy. As a student, she was deeply concerned with issues of discrimination and social justice, and also participated in anti-nuclear demonstrations. To how many out of 100 people who are like Linda do the following statements apply?
Please rank order the following statements with respect to their probability:	Linda is a bank teller
Linda is a bank teller[a]	Linda is a bank teller and active in the feminist movement
Linda is a bank teller and active in the feminist movement	

[a]For both versions, several other statements had to be judged as well (e.g., "Linda is a psychiatric social worker"), but the crucial comparison is between the two statements listed above. For any two categories, A and B, instances of A should be judged more frequent than instances of A&B. In the above case, there are more bank tellers than there are bank tellers who are feminists, because the category "bank tellers" includes both feminists and non-feminists.

duplicated Cosmides's results, but they offer a different explanation of those results. While agreeing that the associationism-based familiarity and the pragmatic reasoning schema hypotheses are false (or likely false), they argue that there are two possible explanations of Cosmides's results. One is Cosmides's idea that a social contract explains the content effects; the other is that a cheater algorithm explains the content effects. They show that the second view is supported by the data. Cosmides and Tooby have since accepted this friendly amendment by Gigerenzer and Hug.[10]

In a 1996 issue of *Cognition,* Cosmides and Tooby argued that the cases where subjects ignored base rates were all formulated as single-case probability examples. By contrast, if these examples are reconstrued as relative frequency cases, subjects do dramatically better on the same experiments. Similar results have been obtained with respect to the conjunction fallacy by Fieldler (1988), and overconfidence by Gigerenzer, Hoffrage, and Kleinbolting (1991). (For a review, see Gigerenzer 1991.) Consider the data from Fieldler (1988) shown in table 5.2.

Here the conjunction fallacy disappears when subjects are asked for frequencies rather than single-event probabilities. While 70 to 80 percent of subjects commit the conjunction fallacy when asked for single-event probabilities, 70 to 80 percent do not commit this fallacy when asked for relative frequencies. Likewise, Gigerenzer, Hoffrage, and Kleinbolting (1991) found that the overconfidence bias disappears when subjects are asked to judge relative frequencies, as opposed to single-case probabilities. The overconfidence bias occurs when there is a gap between one's degree of belief (confidence) in a single event and the relative frequency with which those events occur. Such a violation is not a violation of frequentist theories of probability, since subjects were, in this case, not judging frequencies. When subjects were judging frequencies, the results showed that subject's judged frequencies were similar to the actual frequencies. As Cosmides and Tooby comment on Gigerenzer et al.: "According to their probabilistic mental model theory, one's confidence in a single answer is an estimate of the ecological validity of the cues used in providing that answer, not an estimate of the long-run relative frequency of correct answers" (Cosmides and Tooby 1996, pp. 19–20). However, by assuming that people extract information from their environment in the form of frequencies, Gigerenzer et al. were able to arrive at well-calibrated performances concerning both overestimation and underestimation. Moreover, there is preliminary evidence from McCauley and Stitt (1978) to suggest that base-rate neglect disappears when subjects are asked for frequencies rather than single-case probabilities.

These data suggest that humans may, after all, be good intuitive inductive reasoners even if they are poor intuitive deductive reasoners. This fact may be explained by noting that inductive reasoning is likely to have been far more important for the survival and replication of the genes of our Pleistocene ancestors than deductive reasoning. The reason for this is that induction-based learning about the environment, though fraught with danger and subject to inferential error, had to be—prima facie—one of the best hedges against disaster that our Pleistocene ancestors possessed.

If this interpretation of the data is even close to the mark then humans do not reason logically, but adaptively. I shall refer to this latter sort of reasoning as "adapticism." The content effects on the Wason selection task can be explained only by appeal to such cheater-detection conditions, not by the subject's familiarity with the material as some have thought. More important, there seem to be no deductive, domain-general, content-neutral reasoning capacities evidenced in humans. Instead, adapticist reasoning capacities that are context- and content-driven seem to be involved. This result is in keeping with the idea of a multimodular mind where each module was fashioned to handle discrete tasks in the local environments where our ancestors found themselves. As Cosmides and Tooby point out:

Modular, domain-specific, or content-specific approaches ultimately derive their rationale from considerations that are either implicitly or explicitly functional and evolutionary.... This is because many families of important adaptive problem can be solved more efficiently by cognitive mechanisms that were specially tailored to meet the particular task demands characteristic of that problem-type (e.g., vision ... ; language-acquisition ... ; the perception and representation of object motion ... ; the representation of biomechanical motion ... ; cooperation [Cosmides, 1989; Cosmides and Tooby, 1989; Gigerenzer and Hug, 1992]). The trade-off between generality of application and efficiency in performance leads to different compromises in different cases, with generality of application by no means always winning out. (Cosmides and Tooby 1996, pp. 63–64)

Cosmides and Tooby go on to suggest that there may be other normative accounts of probability that are enshrined in other modules of the mind that operate on other tasks. The large array of contexts in which our ancestors found themselves, in tandem with their needs, led to a variety of cognitive modules fashioned to deal with specific tasks that they confronted. These tasks seem to have benefited from inductive reasoning mechanisms that were reliable specifically for just those tasks.

The empirical story that I have just outlined is essentially that of Cosmides and Tooby, but theirs is not the only game in town. The Wason selection task has been described in a recent textbook as "the most intensively researched single problem in the history of the psychology of reasoning" (Evans, Newstead, and Byrne 1993, p. 99). As such, it has become something of an acid test for reasoning theories in the sense that if you cannot explain content effects adequately, then you do not have an adequate reasoning theory. The result is that, in addition to the four positions that I have just outlined, one can discern several other positions in the literature. I prefer Cosmides and Tooby's account, but there are numerous interpretations of the Wason selection task. Aside from the social contract (Cosmides and Tooby), cheater detection (Gigerenzer and Hug, Cosmides and Tooby), pragmatic reasoning schema (Cheng and Holyoak), and associationist views (Wason, Kahneman and Tversky, and Nisbett and Ross), there are at least five other interpretations of the selection task currently on offer. Other than

Gigerenzer and Hug, the view closest to Cosmides and Tooby is that of Denise Cummins (Cummins 1996; Cummins and Allen 1998). In what follows, I will rely on Denise Cummins's excellent summary of these five positions (Cummins 1996).

Like Cosmides and Tooby, Cummins argues that there are innate, domain-specific computational processors involved in human mental architecture. In particular, Cummins argues for the existence of an innate, deontic reasoning module (as opposed to an indicative reasoning module) that emerges early in human development. When reasoning about deontic rules (what one may, should, or should not do in a set of circumstances), reasoners employ a violation-detection strategy. Such reasoners do not adopt this strategy when reasoning about indicative rules (descriptions about purported states of affairs), but, instead, employ a confirmation-seeking strategy. Cummins argues that this deontic/indicative distinction is a primitive in cognitive architecture, that it persists in adulthood, is observed among preliterate societies, and has its counterpart among a range of nonhuman primates. This latter fact suggests that such reasoning has its roots not in the Pleistocene period as Cosmides and Tooby suggest, but much earlier in the hominid-diversifying Miocene period.

Cummins offers the following evidence for her view that there is an innate, domain-specific, deontic module in human mental architecture. Prefrontal lobe syndrome is a pattern of impaired reasoning performance that results from bilateral damage to the ventromedial prefrontal cortical lobes (Damasio 1994). Prefrontal syndrome, Cummins thinks, constitutes the "smoking gun" that shows definitively that social reasoning can be dissociated selectively from other types of reasoning at the neurological level (Cummins 1996). This results in an inability to respond properly to the social rules that underlie the dominance hierarchy of primate social structures. As Damasio puts it: "It is fair to say that monkeys with prefrontal damage can no longer follow the complex social conventions characteristic of the organization of a monkey troop (hierarchical relations of its different members, dominance of certain females and males over other members, and so on)" (1994, p. 75). It is on this basis that Cummins suggests that deontic reasoning constitutes an innate, domain-specific module. Moreover, the intricate dominance hierarchies involved in primate social structure suggest that such domain-specificity has its roots in very early hominid history, namely, the Miocene period. Though Cummins picks out a different time frame (Miocene vs. Pleistocene) and a different context (deontic vs. so-cial exchange) than Cosmides and Tooby, her work builds on the idea of cheater detection that Cosmides and Tooby endorse. Hence, her work rep-resents a friendly contribution to the work of Cosmides and Tooby.[11]

A second view is that of Braine, O'Brien, Rips, and Osherson. They argue that human reasoning is based on the activation of syntax-sensitive rules, and content effects reflect factors outside the rule-base itself (Braine 1978; Braine and O'Brien 1991; Braine, Reiser, and Rumain 1984; Rumain, Con-nell, and Braine 1983; Osherson 1975; Rips 1983, 1994). To explain the con-tent effects on the Wason selection task these authors have been forced to add content-sensitive parameters (Braine and O'Brien 1991) or modal oper-ators (Rips 1983, 1994) to their reasoning systems. But, as Cummins points out, this concedes the point that syntax-sensitive rules are inadequate to explain content effects (Cummins 1996). This view is, of course, completely at odds with that of Cosmides and Tooby and Cummins in the sense that a domain-general, content-neutral psycho-logic is posited, which is supple-mented by factors outside the rule base in order to explain content effects. This sort of solution, as Cummins intimates, seems ad hoc.

A third view is that of Manktelow and Over (1990, 1991, 1995). They at-tribute the preference for violation-detecting strategies concerning prob-lems with deontic contents to the construction of mental models based on social roles and subjective utility. They think deontic reasoning is psycho-logically distinct from indicative reasoning. In the former, where one is con-cerned about what one may or must do, one is focused on the subjective utility of possible outcomes of one's actions. In the latter, one is focused on actual states of affairs and the truth of sentences describing such states. They study the former sort of case and argue that the perspective taken and the subjective utility assigned to possible outcomes in deontic reasoning problems using the Wason selection task determines the performance of subjects (Manktelow and Over 1991). This view is not necessarily at odds with Cummins's view in that Manktelow and Over may just be filling in im-portant details concerning the nature of the innate, domain-specific deon-tic modules that she posits. In fact, it seems possible that Cosmides and Tooby could endorse their view but attribute the details to an innate, Dar-winian algorithm that operates in domain-specific social-contract settings. Hence, this position can be seen as building on the work of evolutionary psychologists such as Cosmides and Tooby.

A fourth view is Oaksford and Chater's rational analysis (1994, 1998). They offer an analysis of performance on the indicative, abstract reasoning and the deontic, thematic reasoning versions of the Wason selection task based on information theory (Shannon and Weaver 1949; Wiener 1948) (see 3.2 for more on information theory), Bayesian decision making, and subjective utility. Indicative rule-testing is modeled as hypothesis-testing under conditions of uncertainty where the reasoner chooses experiments, that is, card turnings on the Wason selection task, based on the amount of information that the experiment is likely to provide. Rational decision making is defined as choosing to turn cards on the Wason selection task that are expected to lead to the greatest reduction in uncertainty, or the greatest information gain. The reduction in uncertainty concerns which of two hypotheses is true, that is, "if p is true, then q must be true too" or "p and q are independent." When the incidences of p and q are low in the sample space (rarity condition), then the ordering of information gain for each of the four standard cards in the selection task is $p > q >$ not-$q >$ not-p. This explains why reasoners prefer to turn the q rather than the not-q card. As Cummins points out: "As the probabilities associated with the incidences of p and q increase, so does the information value associated with selecting the not-q card. In contrast, selection performance on deontic versions of the selection task is explained using the same probabilistic model coupled with the assignment of different subjective utilities to each card depending on the viewpoint that is adopted during reasoning. Rational decision-making is defined in this case as selecting cards that maximize expected utility" (1996, p. 179). The result is that a violation-detection strategy develops here since the model predicts that violating instances have the greatest expected utility. Domain-dependent changes in selection performance result from domain-specific knowledge that influences the parameters in the model (ibid., p. 180). Hence, we get a proposal about what might be inside the deontic reasoning module. Of course, Oaksford and Chater do not offer an evolutionary story, and they actually deny that one is needed. In that sense, their work is not sympathetic to evolutionary psychology.

The fifth and final view is due to Sperber, Cara, and Girotto (1995). They argue that Sperber and Wilson's (1986) relevance theory and Evans's (1989) appeal to relevance can be used to explain the content effects on the Wason selection task. Further, they suggest that the selection task is not a conditional reasoning task in the deductive sense as originally thought by Wason,

Johnson-Laird, and Rips, nor is it a hypothesis evaluation task as thought by Evans (1982). The Wason selection task is simply a task of selecting relevant evidence, and that is what subjects do. Hence, Sperber et al. focus on the psychological processes that guide the selection of information relevant to inferential processes. The idea is that relevant information has the highest cognitive effects for the least processing effort. They develop experiments intended to vary the cognitive effects and the processing efforts needed to solve the selection task. The strategy subjects use on the Wason selection task is to infer directly testable consequences from the rule. They infer consequences in order of their accessibility, and they stop when an interpretation of the rule meets their expectations of relevance. Subjects then select the cards that test the consequences they have inferred from the rule. The order of accessibility of consequences and expectations of relevance vary with rule and context, and, as a result, so does performance.

In the words of Sperber, Cara, and Girotto: "[We] will argue, pragmatic processes of comprehension automatically involve determining where relevance lies, and they serve us rather well in this respect in ordinary life. When subjects fail at the task, it is because of over-confidence in these pragmatic processes, and in the intuition of relevance that they determine. When most subjects succeed at a particular version of the task, it is because the pragmatics of that version are such as to elicit intuitions of relevance that happen to yield logically correct selections" (1995, p. 44). Consider a deontic, thematic rule such as: "If a person is drinking beer, then the person must be over nineteen years of age." In this case, "p" and "q" refer to an "individual drinking beer" and "over nineteen years of age," while "p" and "(not-q)" refers to an "individual drinking beer" and "under nineteen years of age." On the effort side, both are equally easy to represent. On the effect side, adult beer drinking is a trivial event (according to the authors!) whereas underage drinking is socially and morally significant. If one is a law-enforcer, then underage drinking requires of one that they act to sanction it in some way, while no such sanction exists for lawful adult beer drinkers. This is typical of a deontic version of the Wason selection task that results in good performance. In such cases, the "p and (not-q)" case is linguistically highlighted and easier to represent than all the other cases. We tend to have many terms for law-violators but few for law-abiding folk. Their claim is that the experiments they ran and a reinterpretation of numerous experiments of others in the field support the relevance view and disprove other explanations of the selection task.

Sperber, Cara, and Girotto do not rule out a Cosmides-style evolutionary explanation in terms of innate, domain-specific deontic modules. Rather, the claim is that the relevance-theoretic model is more general (it has broader scope) and is to be preferred on these grounds (1995, p. 88). In fact, they argue that the relevance model is not a reasoning model and that the Wason selection task cannot help us discriminate between theories of reasoning. This is so because the content effects on the Wason selection task are largely the result of pragmatically infelicitous formulations, where "q" is not inferable from "p." Put otherwise, when subjects fail to make the logically correct selection, this is owing to stimuli that fail to be optimally relevant and so intuitions "go the wrong way." Be this as it may, and as Sperber et al. admit, their results do not show that Cosmides and Tooby's claim— that there are innate, domain-specific deontic, Darwinian processors—is false. In this sense, the Sperber account is not incompatible with the work of Cosmides and Tooby.

To summarize, a number of authors have supported the view that human reasoning is domain specific and that deontic reasoning crucially depends on violation detection. These authors include Cheng and Holyoak (1985, 1989), Cheng, Holyoak, Nisbett, and Oliver (1986), Cosmides (1989) and Cosmides and Tooby (1994), Manktelow and Over (1991, 1995), Oakesford and Chater (1994, 1998), Sperber, Cara, and Girotto (1995), and Cummins (1996). Others have argued for an evolutionary foundation for such domain-specific reasoning. These authors include Cosmides (1989), Cosmides and Tooby (1994), and Cummins (1996). And although they do not explicitly endorse an evolutionary explanation of these results, the accounts of Sperber, Cara, and Girotto (1995) and Manktelow and Over (1991, 1995) are compatible with such a view. Finally, Cosmides and Tooby (1994) argue for the Pleistocene period as the evolutionary source of many central adaptations, including the cheater detection module. In contrast, Cummins (1996) traces the same adaptations back to the earlier, hominid-diversifying Miocene period. I hope these data give the reader some idea of the evidence concerning domain-specificity and evidence supporting the claim that deontic reasoning crucially depends on violation detection. As the same time, it is important to notice that there is an ongoing literature that develops several alternative positions. That said, on the assumption that the framework and results of evolutionary psychology are—for the most part—on the right track, I want now to explore the likely epistemic implications of evolutionary psychology.

Epistemological Implications

If we mean by "logic" a content-neutral, domain-general, truth-preserving abstract system for which we have soundness and completeness results, then it is very doubtful that the mind embodies anything like a logic system. As some logicians are quick to point out, on this sort of definition, inductive logic is not a logic either. For these reasons, I have urged that our reasoning capacities should be referred to as adapticist. This term better captures the Darwinian roots of our actual reasoning capacities. We need now to consider the implications of mental adapticism for the meliorative project of providing advice to cognizers intent on acquiring significant empirical truths. A first step toward providing a viable solution to the meliorative issue would be for those working on such issues in the epistemology of science to adopt a psychological realism constraint. That is, we ought to endorse meliorative norms that are within the abilities of humans to approximate. The recognition by Bayesians that priors figure in conditionalization contexts represents an improvement in this direction. By this I mean that Bayesian decision theorists maintain that we cannot use a purely objective probability theory, as Carnap did, to arrive at a normative model of scientific decision making. Bayesians offer a "personal" or "subjective" model of probability in that they begin with the individual probability estimates of cognizers and then apply Bayes's theorem to such prior probability estimates in light of incoming data. This is called "conditionalizing" on the data.

The idea is that the addition of the data to the initial probability estimates will eventually produce objective estimates of the likelihood of some event. This differs from Carnap's frequency model by not assuming that the initial probability of an event is 0.5. That is, it differs from Carnap's conception of probability by assuming that cognizers accord some degree of belief to hypotheses independent of the data. Bayesians believe that everyone has a specific subjective probability (degree of belief) for every proposition they can formulate. Here is a simple version of Bayes's theorem:

$$P(h/e) = p(h) \times p(e/h) / p(e)$$

As applied to hypotheses, this says that the probability of a hypothesis given the evidence, e, is equal to the prior probability of the hypothesis times the probability of the evidence given the hypothesis, divided by the probability of the evidence. Clearly, this is an advance over an objectivist, inductivist Carnap-style measure in that it seems to better capture how humans actually think about probability. Carnap, of course, would respond that he is simply providing a purely normative account of how scientists ought to reason, and so it is no criticism to be told that scientists regularly fail to live up to his norms.

But this response will not do, any more than it would be appropriate for an analytic epistemologist to say that it is too bad if no humans live up to her account of epistemic justifiedness. Why? Beyond the embarrassment of providing epistemic advice that even the best scientists did not follow and, as a result, rendering the history of science irrational, the problem is that such advice is sterile. If no one can follow it, then it is epistemically inert and cannot do the job it was designed to do, that is, help us epistemically. We must pursue epistemic norms that are within the capacities of humans to approximate. This point holds both for the task of conceptual analysis and for the meliorative project. For both projects, "ought" implies "can."

Assuming that those working on inductive logic accept the psychological realism constraint, what follows concerning the empirical literature that I have canvased? Assuming a modular mind where each module was fashioned to handle discrete tasks in the local environments of our ancestors, inductivists should look for norms that are tied to specific capacities. If Cosmides and Tooby are right when they suggest that different normative accounts of probability are enshrined in different modules of the mind tied to specific tasks, then the idea of an overarching inductive logic is bound to fail. I am assuming here that the notion of epistemic advice that we are seeking is writ large. That is, we are concerned with epistemic advice not just for the scientist but for the full range of epistemic agents involved in the full range of human inquiries. The prospects for a unified epistemology are, in this sense, bleak. A modular mind is not a mind from which we should expect a unified meliorative solution. Our best science tells us that we should not expect this. Likewise, our account of nonmeliorative justification and knowledge should not be unified. It is entirely possible that the

failure of epistemologists to discover a set of necessary and sufficient conditions for justifiedness or knowledge may be partly attributable to the fact
that human knowledge, insofar as it exists, is parasitic on a modular, adapticist mind. Such a mind was fashioned by the standard evolutionary constraints of natural selection, mutation, migration, and random genetic
drift.

This suggests that we need to think of knowledge as a set of natural kinds
or an empirical phenomenon, rather than a conceptual kind. The conditions governing such natural kinds will vary depending on which modular
mental capacity is at issue. Our native mental architecture gives rise to the
phenomenon of knowledge, and that phenomenon must reflect the capacities that subserve it. Since this is the case, we cannot uncover a univocal
phenomenon that is knowledge or justification. Knowledge and justification (in its meliorative and nonmeliorative guise) are radically fragmented.
We need to get clear on the varieties of nonmeliorative justification in order
to see the structure of different types of modular knowledge and to set the
stage for adequate accounts of meliorative justification. My general message
here is that epistemology must go modular. If epistemology is ever to regain
its intellectual credibility, then epistemologists must respect the facts, as we
know them, concerning our native abilities.

5.3   Conclusion

On my view, there are normative issues in epistemology. But there are no
purely normative issues. What this means is that the norms we fashion
must be reasonable extensions of the capacities that humans possess, keyed
to the local environments in which we find ourselves. One lesson from the
demise of logical positivism should have been that we need epistemic
norms that we can approximate. The mere fact that we can formulate a
norm does not establish that, as a species, we can satisfy, or even approximate, its dictates. Another lesson that we can learn from the failure of
Kuhnian historicism is that we still need epistemic norms. Finally, the failure of recent analytic epistemology to provide a unified account of justifiedness and knowledge can be traced to the fact that the cognitive
architecture of the human mind is modular. We need an analysis of the phenomenon of knowledge that cuts nature at its joints. In the case of human
knowledge, those joints are composed largely of modules in a massively

modular mind. What is needed to transform the traditional project of conceptual analysis and the meliorative project is an epistemology that reflects the modular, adapticist mental capacities of our species in our native environments. In chapter 6, I attempt to provide exactly this sort of modular epistemology. Additionally, I argue that we should reject nonnaturalism because knowledge is not a conceptual kind but, rather, a set of natural kinds. The goal is to provide a truly naturalized epistemology.

6   The Fragmentation of Knowledge

The invasion of science into the pristine labyrinth of analytic epistemology has not been without its detractors. Richard Feldman and Richard Fumerton have been prominent among those that deny that normative issues concerning justification and knowledge can be usefully informed by the descriptive resources of science.[1] On the other hand, among those who wish to naturalize epistemology, there is disagreement as to how science should be utilized to inform matters epistemic. Goldman sees epistemic terms as part of a folk epistemic conceptual apparatus that we need to begin with, and improve on, by constructing a scientific epistemology. Kornblith believes that knowledge is not a concept but a natural kind much like water or aluminium. Papineau thinks that knowledge might be a module in the mind.[2]

As a naturalist, I agree that science must play an important role in clarifying normative, evaluative epistemic terms in nonnormative, descriptive terms. And, as should be obvious by now, I also think that a properly naturalized epistemology must be squared with the latest results from empirical psychology. In this chapter, I hope to contribute to this latter project by integrating the twin ideas that knowledge is modular and that knowledge is constituted by a set of natural kinds with results from evolutionary and nonevolutionary psychology. I shall argue that "strict knowledge" is radically fragmented across a plethora of innate, Chomsky modules or is the result of learning. But before I develop such a modular epistemology, I want to clear the ground by offering an argument against nonnaturalists who argue that science has no place in epistemology.

6.1   Against Nonnaturalism

The central claim by nonnaturalists has been that epistemic issues are essentially normative in nature. As such, the descriptive resources of science are simply irrelevant for the purpose of clarifying normative issues concerning the nature of justification, the conditions governing knowledge, and giving an account of rationality or conceptual change. The fear is that naturalizing epistemology will rob it of its distinctively human aspect; something valuable will be lost—the normative dimension. Naturalists have responded that providing an account that explicates the normative in terms of the nonnormative does not make such epistemic concepts nonnormative.[3] But nonnaturalists have not been impressed.

What I find strange indeed is the idea that human knowledge should stand apart from our analysis of the rest of nature and from our understanding of other species' knowledge. We are to believe that the results of science can have no bearing on the pristine conceptual results of analytic epistemology. We stand alone as epistemologists, providing the a priori foundations of the sciences, and remain unsullied with empirical taint. This picture of the philosopher may seem appealing to arcane ears, steeped in Platonic pedantry, but is it even vaguely defensible today? I doubt it. Philosophy tried to secure a unique role for itself in the last century by sealing itself off from the sciences, with disastrous results. Philosophers such as the later Wittgenstein and J. L. Austin believed that if one simply attended to the nuances of one's native language and remained true to the ordinary meanings of words in standard contexts, many philosophical problems could be resolved. Wittgenstein also argued that philosophers should not appeal to the results of psychology, since appeal to factual, or descriptive, empirical data could not possibly help to solve nonfactual, or purely normative, philosophical problems. One problem with this approach was that ordinary language turned out to be very difficult to analyze in any fruitful, consistent way. Another problem was that the stricture against psychologizing left philosophers ignorant of many important results in the sciences. The result was that ordinary language philosophy was put to rest by the 1950s. Surely, we do not want to repeat that sort of mistake again. But the current disrepute in which analytic epistemology is held can be attributed largely to the insistence of those who would seal epistemology off from science so that the old wheel-spinning, scholastic projects can proceed apace. Despite the success of externalist and reliabilist accounts of justification and knowledge, it would seem that old projects die hard, no matter how unsuccessful they have been.

At the core of the debate, I think, is the assumption that knowledge is a conceptual kind and not a natural kind. If knowledge were a conceptual kind then a priori appeals to reason would seem to be sufficient to elucidate the notion (though Goldman would disagree with nonnaturalists on this point). But if this is not so then science would necessarily be important for the clarification of knowledge as a natural kind. My strategy, polemics aside, will be to demonstrate that knowledge is composed of a set of natural kinds. Eventually, I will suggest that there is a plethora of knowledge modules, each of which is a natural kind. Moreover, much work has already been done in evolutionary and nonevolutionary psychology to clarify these notions. First, let me lay out an argument that, I think, is decisive in establishing that knowledge is a natural kind.

6.2 The "Knowledge Is a Natural Kind" Argument (NKA)

Here is the NKA argument:

1. Either knowledge exists or knowledge does not exist. (Assumption)
2. If knowledge exists, it is either a conceptual kind or a natural kind. (Assumption)
3. If knowledge does not exist, then skepticism is true. (Assumption)
4. Skepticism is false. (Assertion)
5. Knowledge exists. (3,4 MT or 1,4 DS)
6. Knowledge is a conceptual kind or a natural kind. (2,5 MP)
7. If knowledge is a conceptual kind, then it is a social construct. (Assertion)
8. If knowledge is a social construct, then epistemic relativism is true. (Assertion)
9. Epistemic relativism is false. (Assertion)
10. Knowledge is not a social construct. (8,9 MT)
11. Knowledge is not a conceptual kind. (7,10 MT)
12. Therefore, knowledge is a natural kind. (6,11 DS)

My strategy in constructing this argument is to appeal to premises that analytic epistemologists should find compelling, despite a conclusion that they would prefer to reject. The argument will be successful if analytic epistemologists fail to find fault with its premises. I take premise 1 to be noncontroversial. I take premise 2 to exhaust the significant ways in which analytic epistemologists have characterized knowledge. Premise 3 seems straightforwardly true. Most analytic epistemologists would assent to premise 4, that is, Barry Stroud, Peter Unger, et al. aside. For me, and for most analytic epistemologists, skepticism is a last resort or an interesting challenge to those who might defend some account of knowledge. Hence, I will say no more about it here. Premise 5 follows from 3 and 4 by modus tollens. Interestingly, premise 5 also follows from 1 and 4 by disjunctive syllogism. Premise 6 follows from 2 and 5 by modus ponens. Premise 7 is correct because knowledge is normally taken to be a human construct by analytic epistemologists in the sense that it is our concept—we made it. Just as we created the idea of a Canadian quarter, the argument goes, we created the concept of knowledge. Surely premise 8 seems true in the sense that social constructs vary across cultures. By analogy, what counts as a quarter varies across nations. Since that is true, what counts as knowledge similarly varies. But since analytic epistemologists have always wanted to assert that the concept of knowledge is univocal, it follows straightaway that epistemic relativism is false and so premise 9 is true.

Epistemic relativism, as I am using it, is the view that there is no single concept of knowledge shared across cultures. In other words, what counts, and should count, as the concept of knowledge varies from culture to culture. The project of analytic epistemology crucially depends on the falsity of epistemic relativism. After all, there is no point hunting for necessary and sufficient conditions for the concept of knowledge if knowledge is not a single concept. The very idea that our pretheoretic intuitions can be used to adjudicate between competing accounts of knowledge, regardless of where we live, presupposes the falsity of epistemic relativism. In this sense, the methodology of analytic epistemology presupposes the falsity of epistemic relativism. Premise 10 follows from 8 and 9 by modus tollens. Premise 11 follows from 7 and 10 by modus tollens. Finally, the conclusion follows from 6 and 11 by disjunctive syllogism. If I am right, most analytic epistemologists should find each of the premises in this argument to be plausible, since these premises state intuitions that, in my experience, analytic epistemologists share. But the conclusion, in sharp contrast, is one that few analytic epistemologists will welcome. Nevertheless, the argument is deductively valid and so the conclusion follows from these individually plausible premises.

I want now to confront potential objections to the NKA argument. One might worry that I have constructed a false dilemma at premise 2. It might be the case, the argument goes, that knowledge is an artifactual kind or no kind of kind at all. If that were so, then the conclusion clearly would not follow. The burden here, I would argue, is on those who would distinguish between conceptual kinds and artifactual kinds. How, exactly, do these kinds differ? A conceptual kind, on my view, is an a priori product of the human imagination. We create our concepts. These include bachelors, dollar bills, and voting ballots (though not dimpled voting ballots!). We might not have created such concepts at all, or we might have created concepts that were similar to those that we now employ in our conceptual scheme. Our conceptual scheme is both arbitrary and contingent. But what are artifactual kinds? At best, they are simply instantiations of our concepts. The voting ballot that you confront in Palm Beach County in Florida, on election day, is not really a butterfly or a crossword puzzle, though it may appear to be one or the other of these objects. Instead, it is a physical instantiation of a human-made concept. As such, artifactual kinds are derived from conceptual kinds.

The other possibility countenanced by my potential critic is that knowledge is not a kind of kind at all. But what, then, is knowledge? The skeptic's answer is that there is no knowledge. But this, on most versions of skepticism, does not eliminate the notion of knowledge; it merely denies that the concept has an extension. As such, the concept remains intact. Here it seems the burden of the argument is on my critic to clarify what knowledge is. If it is not a human creation, that is, a concept, or a natural kind or even an artificial kind, then I must confess I begin to lose my grip on what is being talked about. Call this the "mystery" notion of knowledge.[4] I find no reason to take seriously the idea that there are alternatives to those mentioned in premise 2 and so I think premise 2 is reasonable.

The other premise that might elicit debate is premise 7. One might wonder whether it is true that conceptual kinds are really social constructs. After all, the argument goes, you claim that the idea of a Canadian quarter is a conceptual kind, but surely Canadian quarters are not social constructs. But notice the legerdemain here: the sentence begins with talk of a conceptual kind, that is, the idea of a Canadian quarter, and ends with talk of an artifactual kind, that is, Canadian quarters. Let me be clear: Canadian quarters (the object) are derived from the idea of a Canadian quarter (even if they now have more in common with the American dime). Once this confusion is cleared up we can see that there is no reason to think that conceptual kinds are not social constructs. Since we create conceptual kinds it follows, ex hypothesi, that conceptual kinds are social constructs. There just is nothing else that conceptual kinds could be.

Knowledge, apparently, is not a conceptual kind. As such, much of traditional epistemology can be put to rest. In addition, those naturalists who suppose that knowledge is a conceptual kind cannot simply assume that this is so. They need to argue for their view. In this respect, Alvin Goldman and Fred Dretske, who helped usher in the epistemological naturalist revolution that we are now experiencing, must be seen as transitionary figures. Why? The answer is that they have not accepted the full implications of their own work since they persist in seeing knowledge as a conceptual kind. As such, they are like Copernicus offering a profoundly new result while remaining wedded to the methodology of the previous paradigm. In the scientific revolution, it was Kepler who introduced the new methodology for astronomy. In the epistemological revolution, it is people like Devitt, Millikan, Stich, and Kornblith who have introduced a new methodology by insisting that knowledge is a natural kind.[5] This is so for the obvious reason that natural kinds must be studied empirically, whereas conceptual kinds can be made perspicuous (it would seem) by appeal to reason alone.

But what is a natural kind? What sort of natural kind is knowledge? Is there a knowledge module just as there is a theory of mind module (ToM) or a folk psychology module or a folk physics module? Are such modules actually natural kinds? If so, is there a knowledge module that is a natural kind, or many knowledge modules, or is knowledge a set of natural kinds? The questions come quickly once we reconfigure knowledge as a natural kind and, subsequently, epistemology as an empirical discipline. Eventually, I will argue that knowledge is not a single natural kind but a set of natural kinds housed in the modules of a massively modular mind. But first, let's begin with the question of what constitutes a natural kind.

6.3   Natural Kinds

Let me be profoundly unoriginal here and side with Kornblith by arguing that Richard Boyd's account of natural kinds is essentially correct. As Kornblith puts it:

Following Richard Boyd, I take natural kinds to be homeostatically clustered properties, properties that are mutually supporting and reinforcing in the face of external change. Consider the case of water. Water is just H_2O. Why does H_2O count as a natural kind? Two atoms of hydrogen and one of oxygen unite to form a homeostatic cluster. The chemical bond, that joins these atoms provides the newly formed unit with a degree of stability that is not found in just any random collection of atoms. The chemical world is divided into kinds by nature precisely because only certain combinations of atoms yield such stable units. In the case of water, as with other natural kinds, the properties that are ultimately responsible for this homeostatic unity are also responsible for a wide range of the kind's characteristic properties. The reason natural kinds support inductive inference is that the properties that are homeostatically clustered play a significant causal role in producing such a wide range of associated properties, and in thereby explaining the kind's characteristic interactions. It is for this reason too that natural kinds figure so prominently in causal laws: laws operate over well-behaved categories of objects, and it is the homeostatic clustering of properties that explains why natural kinds are so well behaved. (2002, pp. 61–62)

If knowledge is a natural kind it follows that the microstructure of knowledge is composed of necessary properties that are conjoined in a homeostatic cluster. The epistemic bond that holds true beliefs together is justification. To a first approximation, one might offer a natural kind version of Goldman's reliable process account of knowledge from "What Is Justified Belief?" by suggesting that the individually necessary, and jointly sufficient, properties of the natural kind that is knowledge constitute a set that is such that:

<S knows that p> iff

1. p is true.

2. S believes that p.

3. S's belief that p is justified in the sense that it is caused by a reliable process and there is no reliable process that could have been used such that, had it been used, it would have undermined S's belief that p.

Note that a process is reliable, on this account, if and only if it tends to produce the truth. The notion of probability implicit in "tends" here is a propensity account of probability. I am not going to defend this natural kind version of (part of) Goldman's reliable process account of knowledge against a variety of (natural kind versions of) well-known objections to Goldman's account, because it is not the account that I will eventually defend. Instead, given this provisional account of the phenomenon of knowledge (not the concept of knowledge), I want to ask the following question. How is this natural kind made evident in humans and what role does it play in the mental architecture of humans? To answer these two questions, I want to introduce some ideas from evolutionary psychology.

6.4   The Massive Modularity Hypothesis (MMH)

As I have indicated in this book, Leda Cosmides and John Tooby have argued that the mind is composed of a "constellation of specialized mechanisms that have domain-specific procedures, operate over domain-specific representations, or both" (Cosmides and Tooby 1994, p. 94). The mind is composed of a set of innate, domain-specific computational mechanisms. As they most floridly put it:

Our cognitive architecture resembles a confederation of hundreds or thousands of functionally dedicated computers (often called modules) designed to solve adaptive problems endemic to our hunter-gatherer ancestors. Each of these devices has its own agenda and imposes its own exotic organization on different fragments of the world. There are specialized systems for grammar induction, for face recognition, for dead reckoning, for construing objects and for recognizing emotions from the face. There are mechanisms to detect animacy, eye direction, and cheating. There is a "theory of mind" module . . . a variety of social inference modules . . . and a multitude of other elegant machines. (Tooby and Cosmides 1995, p. xiv)

Evolutionary psychologists think that the mind is largely composed of Darwinian modules. A module, on this view, is a computational processor somewhat like the Fodorian picture in *The Modularity of Mind* (1983). In that book, Fodor argued that modules are computational processors of a very specific sort in that each module has at least six properties, namely, information encapsulation, mandatoriness, speed, shallow input, neural localization, and susceptibility to characteristic breakdown. Moreover, only input systems (responsible for perception and language processing) and output systems (responsible for action) are modular on his account. Central systems such as those responsible for reasoning and belief fixation are nonmodular.

As Sperber once noted: "Although this was probably not intended and has not been much noticed, 'modularity of mind' was a paradoxical title, for, according to Fodor, modularity is to be found only at the periphery of the mind. . . . In its center and bulk, Fodor's mind is decidedly nonmodular. Conceptual processes—that is, thought proper—are presented as a holistic lump lacking points at which to carve" (1994, p. 39). In contrast, evolutionary psychologists, such as Jackendoff, have argued that: "central capacities too can be divided into domain-specific modules" (Jackendoff 1992, p. 70). As Samuels, Stich, and Tremoulet put it:

So, for example, the linguist and cognitive neuroscientist, Steven Pinker, has suggested that not only are there modules for perception, language and action, but there may also be modules for many tasks traditionally classified as central processes, including:

Intuitive mechanics: knowledge of the motions, forces, and deformations that objects undergo . . . Intuitive biology: understanding how plants and animals work . . . Intuitive psychology: predicting other people's behaviour from their beliefs and desires . . . [and] Self-concept: gathering and organizing information about one's value to other people, and packaging it for others. (Pinker, 1994, p. 420)

According to this view, then, "the human mind . . . [is] not a general-purpose computer but a collection of instincts adapted for solving evolutionarily significant problems—the mind as a Swiss Army knife" (Pinker, 1994). (Samuels, Stich, and Tremoulet 1998, p. 150)

As mentioned in chapter 1, there are ambiguities concerning the massive modularity hypothesis. For instance, what role, if any, does innate knowledge play when a domain-specific computational module is activated? Cosmides and Tooby have committed themselves to the view that we should allow for, and expect, a variety of possibilities to obtain. However, they do think that the mind is largely composed of Darwinian/Chomsky modules.

Richard Samuels has argued against Cosmides and Tooby's view, misconstrued as the claim that the mind is composed *only* of a set of domain-specific, computational processors. He thinks their view fails because there are equally good reasons to think that we employ a domain-general processor with a library model of cognition (LMC), that is, a set of innate, domain-specific bodies of knowledge. As Samuels quotes Carey and Spelke:

Human reasoning is guided by a collection of innate domain-specific systems of knowledge. Each system is characterized by a set of core principles that define the entities covered by the domain and support reasoning about those entities . . . . Humans are endowed with domain-specific systems of knowledge such as knowledge of language, knowledge of physical objects, and knowledge of number. Each system of knowledge applies to a distinct set of entities and phenomena. For example, knowledge of language applies to sentences and their constituents; knowledge of physical objects applies to macroscopic material bodies and their behaviour, and knowledge of number applies to sets and to mathematical operations such as addition. (Samuels 1999, p. 8, quoting Carey and Spelke 1994, p. 169)

Samuels goes on to note that psychologists are often unclear as to what they mean by "innate, domain-specific bodies of knowledge." Nevertheless, Samuels claims that Elman et al. (1996) assert that such knowledge constitutes innate systems of mental representations that encode various kinds of information in a way that is truth-evaluable (though not necessarily true). As such, the psychologist's notion of knowledge is clearly much weaker than the analytic epistemologist's notion for the obvious reason that, according to the latter but not the former group, a necessary condition on knowing is that the belief must be true. At any rate, Cosmides and Tooby seem far more flexible than Samuels gives them credit for, since they do not rule out the possibility that there may be a domain-general processor of domain-specific knowledge modules. Perhaps the best way to put this is that they are inclined to accept MMH but that they acknowledge that LMC, or some other model, may well play some limited role in the mind. Their message seems to be that we should look for more precise computational models, models that specify which representations and procedures are at work, but that it is too early to tell what we may find. *Pace* Samuels, they in no way rule out the library model of cognition.

For the reasons mentioned above, I think Samuels simply misunderstands the position of Cosmides and Tooby. Instead, I have suggested that Cosmides and Tooby are committed to the view that the mind is largely composed of Darwinian/Chomskian modules, supplemented by some box B, C, or D modules. Box B modules are domain-general processors operating on Chomsky modules. Box C modules are Darwinian modules operating on domain-general bodies of data. Box D modules are domain-general processors operating on domain-general bodies of data. I called this the *massively modular representation and processor* (MMRP) model of cognition. Assuming, for purposes of argumentation, that MMRP is true, I now want to look at the possible epistemological consequences of adopting this picture of the mind.

6.5   Epistemology and the Massive Modularity Hypothesis

What would a naturalized epistemology that countenanced the twin ideas that knowledge is a set of natural kinds and that knowledge is modular look like in the face of the hypothesis that MMRP is true? That is, if we take the view that the mind is composed of both innate, domain-specific sets of representations and innate, domain-specific computational processors, then how does this square with the idea that knowledge (in the epistemologist's sense) is a modular set of natural kinds? I will argue that a proper subset of our innate, domain-specific sets of representations constitutes such innate, modular, natural kind knowledge. This knowledge will be the result of

Darwinian/Chomskian modules. But, clearly, not all of the representations housed in a domain-specific module will be veridical. Hence, it will not all be knowledge in the strict sense. But, surely, some of it will pass the test. Another important point to notice is that our knowledge, according to MMRP, will be distributed across many hundreds or thousands of modules. Moreover, some of our strict knowledge will not be innate; some of it will be learned by appeal to inductive and deductive inference and by appeal to the sensory modalities. Such empirical knowledge will be the result of Darwinian modules operating on sensory inputs. If knowledge is a set of natural kinds housed in proper subsets of many modules of a massively modular mind, then an analysis of the phenomena of knowledge is possible. Both innate knowledge and empirical knowledge can, I believe, be captured by the following formulation.

We can say that:

<S has MMRP knowledge that p at t> iff:

1. p is true.

2. S believes that p.

3. S's belief that p is Darwinian module–justified, or DM-justified.

But now we need to interpret the third condition on knowledge in more detail. Here is the account of justification:

S's belief that p is DM-justified at t iff:

1. p is caused by a Darwinian module that has been reliably instantiated.

2. There is no other reliable or conditionally reliable Darwinian module available to S that, had it been used by S in addition to the module actually used, would have resulted in S's not believing that p at t.

It should be noted that "reliable instantiation" implies that the module has been triggered in the way that it was historically triggered in the Pleistocene period in which the module was selected for. A module is reliable when a sufficient proportion of its output-beliefs are true regardless of the truth or falsity of its input-beliefs. A module is conditionally reliable when a sufficient proportion of its output-beliefs are true given that its input beliefs are true. Note that the last two notions parallel Goldman's notions of reliability and conditional reliability, but they apply to Darwinian modules. The important point to notice about conditional reliability is that reasoning or memory cannot be expected to produce true belief if, for instance, these modules are applied to false premises. Also, note that I am assuming an MMRP mind. That is, I assume a mind that is composed of innate, domain-specific computational processors, or Darwinian modules, and that sometimes operates over innate, domain-specific bodies of knowledge or Chomsky modules. The mind, then, is largely, though not completely, composed of Darwinian/Chomsky modules. As noted in chapter 1, the mind cannot be entirely composed of these two kinds of modules.

But we can be even more specific concerning the notion of modular reliability. Principle MR from chapter 3 can now be slightly altered by picking out Darwinian modules. Darwinian modular reliability (DMR), then, has it that:

A Darwinian module is reliable if and only if it usually produces successful results in the actual domain (AD = <RF1, L1, T1> and would usually produce successful results in possible domains (PD = <RF1 + ARF, L1, T1 + N> that are relevantly similar to the actual domain.[6]

The domain in which the proper function of a computational module was selected for constitutes its proper domain. The domain in which the computational module that was selected for now operates is called the actual domain (Sperber 1994, p. 51). The actual domain is constituted by the set of relevant facts, RF1, and the laws of nature, L1, that obtain at time T1. A possible domain is an extension of the actual domain that is physically possible relative to the AD given a passage of time, N, altered relevant facts (ARF), and the laws of nature (L1) that are in force.

Notice that justified beliefs, on this account, are such that they can, though they need not, be false. Clearly, it must be possible to have justified though false beliefs. Knowledge, in contrast, requires the truth condition. This account of the phenomenon or natural kind that is knowledge is fully naturalized. That is, knowledge is a component of the architecture of a massively modular mind in the sense that innate knowledge is housed in proper subsets of MMRP modules, while empirical knowledge may be occurrent to the mind, or stored in short- or long-term memory. The account is unique insofar as it describes the actual phenomenon of knowledge as it occurs naturally in the minds of humans. Knowledge, on my view, is not some abstract concept divorced from the daily activities of humans. As I shall soon argue, the true beliefs that are ingredient for knowledge are instrumentally useful for the satisfaction of our biological needs and are, ipso facto, bound up with our evolutionary history. Before I take up these points, I want to confront a problem.

For some, the deep problem with the view that knowledge is a set of natural kinds is that, typically, when one thinks of natural kinds, one thinks of Putnam's water, Kripke's gold, or Kornblith's aluminum examples. From the observational standpoint, these are physical things with a precise, unobservable microstructure. But knowledge does not seem to be like that. Knowledge is observationally nonphysical, the argument goes, so how can it have a chemical or, in any sense, a physical microstructure? There are really two questions being asked here and they need to be separated. The first question is: isn't it the case that all natural kinds display observable physical properties? The second question is: isn't it the case that all natural kinds admit of analysis in terms of a cluster of unobservable, homeostatic microproperties? The answer to the first question is "No." By analogy, carbon atoms are natural kinds, but they do not normally display observable physical properties (individually). But no one would doubt that carbon atoms constitute a natural kind. Hence, we should not doubt the status of knowledge as a natural kind for this sort of reason.[7] The answer to the second question, ex hypothesi, is "Yes." The important point to notice is that natural kinds may be reducible to physical substructures even though the natural kind is itself unobservable.

More generally, for something to count as a natural kind, it must satisfy the following individually necessary and jointly sufficient set of conditions:

A. The properties are mutually supporting and reinforcing in the face of external change (homeostatic properties).

B. These microproperties give rise to the kind's characteristic observable properties by virtue of the causal powers of the micro properties (standard observable effects).

C. Causal laws obtain because the microproperties cause and explain the observable properties of such well-behaved, natural kinds (supports causal laws).

For instance, water is a natural kind. Namely, water just is H_2O. Its microstructure requires that there be two atoms of hydrogen and one atom of oxygen united in a unique chemical bond that produces a stable unit. Condition (A) is satisfied. The microstructure of water gives rise to the characteristic macroproperties that we associate with water. Namely, this stuff is always a tasteless, odorless, colorless liquid. Condition (B) is satisfied. Water will, ceteris paribus, freeze at 32 degrees and boil at 212 degrees Fahrenheit and so on. Condition (C) is satisfied. Hence, water is a natural kind. Such observable regularities portend causal laws. Does knowledge satisfy these constraints? Yes. The homeostatic cluster of properties essential to knowledge is picked out by the three conditions governing knowledge mentioned earlier. That is, knowledge requires belief, truth, and justification. Together, these three properties of knowledge constitute a homeostatic cluster of properties. The model says that the properties in a cluster support and reinforce one another (in the face of external change). Does justification support belief? Yes, there is an obvious sense in which justification provides support for and reinforces belief. After all, what better reason is there to hold a belief other than the fact that one would be justified in so doing?

Does justified belief support and reinforce truth? Yes, the very idea of epistemically justified belief requires that the reason we prefer justified beliefs is that they give us some purchase on truth. Otherwise, it would be unclear why anyone would care about possessing justified beliefs. Analytic epistemologists have long argued that there is, in fact, an analytic—or internal—connection between the justification condition on knowledge and the truth condition on knowledge. As Peter Unger would say, knowledge is not at all accidental. That is because it is a stable, enduring kind in the world. Presumably, it would have been important in our ancestral history to be able to access the truth in a regular, dependable way. In the face of external change or an uncertain environment, dependable truth or knowledge would be a valuable commodity. In this way, justified true belief comes in a package for us even though it is truth that is crucial for our evolutionary success. The path to truth comes by way of justified belief. Now one might wonder at this point: can properties actually have causal influence over each other? That is, can the justification property influence the belief property? The answer is "No"; it is the *objects* that possess such properties or *property instances* that have a causal influence over one another. For instance, it is the fact that certain modules confer justifiedness by virtue of causal relations to specific belief states that makes justified beliefs possible. So, the perceptual module once instantiated provides a causal channel such that, eventually, we may hold justified perceptual beliefs. When such justified belief states embody a property instance of truth, then we have a property instance of knowledge. I hold—quite literally—that knowledge is composed of a cluster of *property instances* that mutually support and reinforce one another. Knowledge is literally a natural kind in the mind.

Does knowledge give rise to standard observable effects? Yes. We can explain much of how we interact socially by positing knowledge. For instance, our verbal behavior evinces much talk of knowledge and truth as when we say things like "Jones is knowledgeable," or "One cannot trust Smith because he is a liar." Knowledge and truth and belief are absolutely crucial organizing principles for social life. They play enormous roles in the shaping of behavior and the satisfaction of our need for food, for flight, to fight, and for sexual reproduction.

Are there causal laws that result from the existence of knowledge? Yes. Knowledge must be reliable and must interact reliably with other desires to regularly produce the satisfaction of our needs and other goals we might have. It is here that we are forced to acknowledge that there is a set of natural kinds that result in a variety of knowledges. This is so because the causal laws that obtain will be specific to each innate, Darwinian/Chomsky module. As such there is no univocal natural kind that is knowledge. This marks a central point in the theory and justifies the move from thinking of knowledge as a single natural kind (as the NKA argument seeks to establish) to thinking of knowledge as constituting a set of natural kinds. This set of strict natural kinds is constitutive of human knowledge; such knowledge is adaptive because it essentially involves true belief. That is, knowledge is causally ingredient to our successful adaptation to the environment that we find ourselves in. Knowledge must, of course, be successfully integrated with our other capacities. But knowledge did, and does, play a necessary causal role in the successful adaptation of humans to their environment. If what I have argued so far is correct, knowledge is a set of natural kinds and natural kinds are homeostatic clusters of properties. Hence, knowledge consists of a set of homeostatic clusters of properties, that is, the conditions on knowledge are actually properties of homeostatic clusters. Moreover, knowledge constitutes a proper subset of an array of MMRP modules. For instance, some strict mathematical knowledge is a proper subset of the mathematics MMRP module. Strict perceptual knowledge is a proper subset of the perceptual MMRP module, and so on. One strength of the account is that it can explain how both innate knowledge and empirical knowledge occur naturally. Just how much innate knowledge exists is an empirical question that I cannot answer here. The important point to notice is simply that the account picks out, and explains the genesis of, this type of knowledge.

However, a problem remains with the idea that the conditions on knowledge constitute a homeostatic cluster of properties of a set of natural kinds. Namely, belief, truth, and justification, although they are unobservable, do not seem to go "deep enough" for the explanation of knowledge since they are nonphysical in nature. What is needed is a suitably biological account of the basis of knowledge. Such an account would uncover the deep, unobservable, physical microstructure of knowledge. A first step in this direction is the endorsement of MMRP as a potential analysis of the role of knowledge in our mental architecture. But even once we make the suggestion that there might be innate, domain-specific sets of representations or bodies of knowledge distributed across modules of the mind, questions remain. For instance, how is such innate knowledge physically realized in the brain? If beliefs are sentences in the head as they are on Fodor's language of thought (LOT) hypothesis then we have the beginnings of an account of such a structure. Of course, there are other models that one might appeal to here. But, at any rate, some such physicalist story is what is required before the idea that knowledge is a set of natural kinds can be given a completely scientific treatment.

6.6   Knowledge and Proper Function

But what is the function of such knowledge? If knowledge is a set of natural kinds located in a variety of proper subsets of MMRP modules, and modules have proper functions, then knowledge plays a role in the execution of such modules' proper function. Roughly, the role of knowledge is to connect us *reliably* to the truth. For instance, the mathematics module's proper function is to acquire mathematical truths. Knowledge plays a role in this process. We might stumble on the truth from time to time, but that would not effectively serve our evolutionary needs in the long run. What is needed is a dependable way of arriving at the truth. Knowledge constitutes just such a dependable connection to the truth by way of justified beliefs. Truth, in turn, is instrumentally useful for the satisfaction of our biological needs for food, flight, fighting, and sexual reproduction. More generally, truth is instrumentally useful for the pursuit of our goals, whatever they may be (see Kornblith 1993). To summarize, knowledge:

1. is a set of natural kinds;

2. is a proper subset of MMRP modules realized in the brain; and

3. plays a role in executing the proper function of the module that it belongs to: its role is to connect humans to the truth *reliably* in ways that support the adaptation of the organism to the environment.

In short, knowledge is a set of natural kinds located in a variety of MMRP modules whose function is to assist modules in the production of true beliefs that enhance the adaptiveness of the organism to its natural environment.

6.7 Knowledge and Spatial Reorientation

With this picture of knowledge in place, we are now in a position to look for evidence for such structures. So, let's consider an example of strict, innate MMRP knowledge. The study by Hermer and Spelke (1996) discussed in chapter 2 is an example not just of abduction, but of natural kind geometric knowledge concerning spatial reorientation. Recall that the study suggests that both adult rats and young children spatially reorient themselves by appeal to an innate, informationally encapsulated, task-specific, modular computational mechanism (Cheng 1986; Cheng and Gallistel 1984). This mechanism appeals to the large-scale shape of the environment but not to the nongeometric properties of the environment. Only geometric properties of the room were appealed to for purposes of spatial reorientation. In contrast, adult humans appeal to both geometric and nongeometric properties of environments to reorient themselves.

Recall that Hermer and Spelke argued that appeal to nongeometric properties may be a late development in humans in one of two ways. That is, either humans become more flexible by overcoming the limitations of appealing only to geometric factors during development, or the original geometric process may persist over cognitive development while new processes are added on. Here, once again, are their words: "As with the systems of knowledge underlying human language, number, reasoning about objects, and social understanding, the core properties of this system of geometric knowledge appear to emerge early in life and to be conserved over human development (Hermer and Spelke 1996, p. 229). (See Gallistel and Gelman 1992 for parallel claims about the system of knowledge of number.)

Hermer and Spelke suggest that common cognitive processes are to be expected across species especially when they are compared at early points in ontogony. Natural selection builds new processes or "terminal additions" on top of existing adaptive traits, and these additions tend to be instantiated late in development. This suggests that the human ability to extend our knowledge into areas for which our biology has not prepared us can be better studied by initially studying early-developing, task-specific mechanisms and later, seeing how further cognitive processes constitute terminal additions to the initial ones to overcome their limitations.

It may be, for instance, that our ability to reflect on the propositions we believe is one such late development that has been useful for problem solving over our evolutionary history. The debate between internalists and externalists over the nature of epistemic justification might, for instance, reflect an awareness of reflective versus nonreflective knowledge in a way that parallels our evolutionary history. That is, the sort of reflective procedures that internalists advocate might represent a terminal addition to the nonreflective procedures that externalists tend to emphasize. It would follow not that there are necessarily two kinds of knowledge evidenced here but that there are two kinds of processes that subserve the acquisition of natural kind knowledges. It may even be that reflective, witting knowledge-acquisition procedures are an attempt to (implicitly) duplicate or mimic, where possible, the nonreflective knowledge-acquisition procedures that reliably produce the sort of knowledge that is the common cognitive coin of many species. If that were so, then one might envision a meliorative project that had us developing subjective epistemic principles and procedures that were the objective epistemic analogues or counterparts of the processes that most species utilize beneath the surface, at a subdoxastic level. For our purposes, what is important to note here is that we possess geometric knowledge in the sense that we innately know that the correct way to spatially reorient ourselves is to appeal to the shape of the environment in which we find ourselves when reorienting. Moreover, we innately know that we should appeal to nongeometric knowledge of the environment when appeals to geometric factors are insufficient to produce correct results concerning where hidden objects in a room might be. That is, spatial reorientation depends on an MMRP module that utilizes a domain-specific, task-specific body of knowledge in conjunction with a domain-specific, task-specific computational mechanism.

My claim is that part of this domain-specific body of representations constitutes strict knowledge in the sense of true, justified beliefs about the environment, about successful reorientation procedures, and about how to find missing objects under such conditions. More generally, the idea is that we possess strict knowledge that parallels such proper subsets of geometric knowledge concerning human language, number, reasoning about objects, and social understanding. Moreover, there is likely to be such strict knowledge housed in a proper subset of many MMRP modules, including folk psychology and many other modules. Such strict knowledge has the evolutionary function of purchasing us the truth. These truths are instrumentally valuable as causal ingredients in the pursuit of our biological needs and the fulfillment of other desires and goals we may have.

However, a problem arises with the previous example. The sort of knowledge canvased is subdoxastic in the sense that the reorientation procedures depend on innate processes. In contrast, some might say that knowledge requires occurrent beliefs. It seems contradictory to require that knowledge is both subdoxastic and doxastic. Isn't such a conception of knowledge incoherent? The answer, I think, is that because some of our strict knowledge is innate, it will be subdoxastic. One might call such knowledge "embedded knowledge" in that such knowledge involves beliefs, but beliefs that are in a sense submerged. Other knowledge is learned, though even learned knowledge can be embedded in that it is stored and so nonoccurrent, and, often, both species of knowledge are involved in our cognitive activities. Note that embedded knowledge is not dispositional knowledge, where dispositional knowledge involves knowing how to do something as opposed to knowing that p is the case. In contrast, embedded knowledge is knowledge that p is the case. My point is simply that embedded knowledge is nonoccurrent. As with many human behaviors, nature and nurture make their distinctive contributions. It should also be reemphasized that the MMRP model of cognition is a picture of both innate and empirical knowledge structures. A final point to note is that some knowledge may be result of box B, box C, or box D modules. A similar analysis would apply to such cases.

6.8   Conclusion

If what I have argued is correct, knowledge is a set of natural kinds housed in many modules, the proper function of which is to deliver the truth to us for the sake of satisfying our biological needs. Such strict knowledge constitutes a proper subset of the innate, domain-specific sets of representations, or is empirical and either occurrent to the mind or stored in short or long-term memory. That's my brief for a fully naturalized epistemology. The place of truth in our cognitive economy should now be clear. The account of knowledge we now have before us is, I think, rife with important implications. In particular, the epistemic relativism that Stich argued for in *The*

Fragmentation of Reason (1990) can now be countered. The path to truth is accessed, in turn, through meliorative justification, nonmeliorative justification, and modular knowledge. That path is underwritten by a plethora of Darwinian modules, often operating in tandem with Chomsky modules. To repeat: the proper function of such knowledge modules is to give us the truth. Truth, in turn, is instrumentally useful for the satisfaction of our four biological needs, the satisfaction of which paves the way for survival and successful reproduction. The knowledge subset of a Chomsky module, in two words, is a Darwinian adaptation. Likewise, of course, Darwinian computational processors are Darwinian adaptations. For brevity, but understood in the way just mentioned, we can say that Darwinian/Chomsky modules are Darwinian adaptations. Once again, it is not particular beliefs or even types of beliefs that are selected for. Rather, it is the modules that give rise to beliefs (where beliefs arise) that are selected for—Darwinian/Chomsky modules.

Truth, on this view, is the central though not the only epistemic goal of science and, indeed, of all human inquiry that is biologically motivated. Of course, humans engage in many nonbiologically based, culturally motivated pursuits. In no way would I dare suggest that my account is the whole story about humans; but I hope it identifies a crucial part of such a story. On my view, humans produce strict knowledge of many different natural kinds in hundreds or thousands of innate, Darwinian/Chomsky modules in the mind. They also produce knowledge through learning. Knowledge is in this sense fragmented, but epistemic relativism does not follow from this. Humans, arguably, are a natural kind. Hence, we universally, as a species, display the same set of natural kind knowledges. There is, then, unity among diversity. What can count as mathematical knowledge will be common among us, and we will bring the same set of skills, for the most part, to bear on mathematical problems. The causal laws that make mathematical knowledge possible are shared among us. The fragmentation of knowledge does not imply epistemic relativism. Nevertheless, the fragmentation of knowledge is a consequence of the fragmentation of reason.

Postscript

Evolutionary psychology has all the advantages and disadvantages of an emerging scientific discipline. It promises a new landscape for understanding human psychology within a biological framework. It promises new connections between old and venerable lines of inquiry. To date, the results have been both stunningly surprising and highly controversial. In this book, I have tied my philosophical wagon to those results. Some may find this to be a mug's game. After all, I might be charged with "scientism" by philosophers just by virtue of adopting a methodology that gives science pride of place. Alternatively, I risk the possibility of making philosophical errors if those scientific results from which I derive philosophical fruit turn out to be false.

I think that neither worry should be of particular concern for the following reasons. "Scientism" is a pejorative label indicating that someone is slavishly wedded to the results of science in an uncritical fashion. But I am not so wedded. As indicated in chapter 5, I think that there are normative issues to be addressed even in a naturalized epistemological framework. In fact, naturalized epistemologists, such as Quine, Goldman, and Stich, are agreed on this point.[1] But where I disagree with internalists and some externalists, such as Goldman and Dretske, is that I believe that knowledge is a set of natural kinds to be studied empirically, not a conceptual kind to be elucidated, primarily, by appeal to reason. The fact that I adopt this view does not make me guilty of scientism any more than Quine's view that there are no analytic statements rendered him guilty of scientism. Since no one would dream of inflicting such an adjective on Quine, I would ask for equal treatment. There is, I would argue, a great deal of room for philosophical analysis even for a naturalist, like myself, who argues that knowledge is a set of natural kinds. Likewise, I think there is a great deal of room for the scientist to engage in conceptual work. Like Quine, I accept the reciprocal containment thesis: there is science in philosophy and philosophy in science. Hilary Kornblith's notion of a weak replacement thesis, in effect, captures Quine's position, though Kornblith argued for a stronger reading of Quine in the introduction to his anthology, *Naturalizing Epistemology*.[2]

As for the charge that I risk negating my own philosophical theory by basing it on a scientific theory that may turn out to be false, I would say the following. Some of the greatest philosophers, for example, Aristotle, Descartes, Hume, and Kant, made the same mistake. How pleasant it would be to enjoy such company. That said, the solution to the disjunction problem involving the gap between the proper and actual domains, which I advanced in chapter 3, is compatible with several varieties of evolutionary psychology. That is fine with me since the "fact of evolution," as Michael Ruse has argued, is not in doubt.[3] Of course, one might doubt whether one could employ the resources of evolutionary theory to reconstruct semantical notions, as I have done. But I addressed that issue, in response to Fodor, for semantical notions in chapter 3. As for the worry that the epistemological results would fall if the MMRP model of cognition were false, here is my response. The project for any naturalized epistemologist is to see how far the results of science can inform matters epistemic. There is a genuine risk involved here, but it is one that must be taken. The alternative, as I mentioned in chapter 1, is the sterile and moribund approach of analytic epistemology. Surely, that approach has been given opportunity enough over the last several hundred years to solve the main problems of epistemology and has failed miserably. In the spirit of the millennium, let's try a new approach and see what we can learn.

I have also committed myself to what might be seen as an unrelenting adaptacism in this book. Some might think that I see Darwinian adaptations under every stone. It is true that I think that human reasoning is an adaptation that, like visual perception, has contributed to our fitness as a species. But, as mentioned in chapter 4, we do not find this claim implausible in the case of visual perception. By analogy, I do not think that we should find the parallel claim implausible in the case of human reasoning. Just as we are subject to the Müller-Lyer illusion, we are subject to content effects on the Wason selection task. We do not think that visual perception is deeply defective, and neither should we think that human reasoning is.

Where we notice central capacities at work in humans, we should expect that natural selection has played its role. As a result, we should look for proper functions that fall out of such central capacities. That much, I take it, is just good science.

I also want to say something about the meliorative project. I have suggested that knowledge is a set of natural kinds housed in subsets of innate, Chomsky modules in a massively modular mind. Alternatively, knowledge may be learned and stored in short- or long-term memory. Finally, knowledge may be occurrent to mind. I have also argued that one needs to answer such metaepistemic questions about knowledge and nonmeliorative justification prior to answering normative-epistemic questions about the meliorative project or applied-epistemic questions about instrumental rationality and the applied norms of, say, science. Moreover, I have advocated the use of a psychological realist constraint on all epistemic theorizing. The upshot of this picture of knowledge is that knowledge is radically fragmented across different modules of the mind and, as such, is governed by different causal laws in each module. The result is that we cannot expect a unified account of the phenomena that constitutes nonmeliorative justification or knowledge. Likewise, we cannot expect a unified meliorative account of justification requisite for the pursuit of inquiry. But I have offered no detailed, positive account of the meliorative project or, indeed, of meliorative justification for any Chomsky module. I take that to be an important and separate project that requires a book-length treatment in its own right. But answering such questions also depends on what evolutionary psychologists tell us about such Chomsky modules. I take it that a great deal of empirical work needs to be done to prepare the ground for work on the meliorative project. At the same time, philosophers of science have been hard at work on normative epistemic questions for a long time. I doubt that anyone can reinvent that wheel. That said, I do believe that the judicious use of evolutionary psychology combined with the perspective on knowledge and representation outlined in the preceding chapters can be of some considerable use in forwarding the meliorative project. I hope to have made the case for that result in this book.

To conclude, I have offered what I take to be a new account of misrepresentation and a new account of knowledge. I have also tried to connect issues in naturalized philosophy of science with issues in analytic epistemology and philosophy of mind. Seeing such connections is, I think, crucial for progress in each domain. Finally, I have based this work on the results of both evolutionary psychology and philosophical analysis. I view these steps in philosophy as being as tentative as the steps that Cosmides and Tooby have made in psychology. Although much work remains in the reconstruction of reason and representation, I hope the position advanced in this book leads us in a new and interesting direction. That direction requires of us that all subsequent epistemological reflection must take its inspiration far more intimately and directly from research and findings in the relevant empirical sciences.

Notes

Chapter 1

1. See, for instance, the *New York Review of Books* (June 12 and 26, 1997), where Stephen J. Gould attacked evolutionary psychology. There is also a churlish reply from Tooby and Cosmides later that year (July 7, 1997). But see also the responses by Dennett (Dennett and Gould 1997) and Pinker (Pinker and Gould 1997). Interesting defenses of evolutionary psychology can be found in Henry Plotkin's *Evolution in Mind* (1997), and Steven Pinker's *How the Mind Works* (1997) and *The Blank Slate* (2002). But evolutionary psychology's primary text is *The Adapted Mind* (1992), edited by Barkow, Cosmides, and Tooby. The most detailed critique of evolutionary psychology to date is Fodor's *The Mind Doesn't Work That Way* (2000), but see also the essays in Fodor's *In Critical Condition* (1998). An excellent anthology on modularity is Hirshfield and Gelman's *Mapping the Mind* (1994).

2. For a discussion by a philosopher about various ways in which science and philosophy can enrich each other, see Alvin Goldman's introduction to *Epistemology and Cognition* (1986).

3. See chapter 5, section 4, where I argue that Richard Samuels misinterprets Cosmides and Tooby by suggesting that they defend the view that the mind consists entirely, or almost entirely, of Darwinian modules. I think their view is more complex than Samuels indicates.

4. Rudolf Carnap famously argued for the unity of science hypothesis in the first volume of *The Unity of Science* (1938).

5. Cosmides and Tooby, of course, intend their project to extend far beyond psychology and biology. In *The Adapted Mind,* they lay out in the preface (with Barkow) a grand synthesis of the natural and behavioral sciences. As they note: "Conceptual integration—also known as vertical integration—refers to the principle that the various disciplines within the behavioral and social sciences should make themselves mutually consistent, and consistent with what is known in the natural sciences as well" (Barkow, Cosmides, and Tooby 1992, p. 4).

6. Gould, however, disagreed with Cosmides and Tooby on many other issues. See the *New York Review of Books* (June 12 and 26, 1997).

7. See Chomsky's book, *Rules and Representations* (1980), for a detailed discussion of such arguments. Also, see Fodor's *The Mind Doesn't Work That Way* (2000), chapter 2, for a description of how Chomsky fits into the New Synthesis or evolutionary psychology. It should also be mentioned that some recent empirical findings are at odds with such poverty of the stimulus arguments. A case in point is the work of Reber and Squire (1999) on subjects' abilities to master artificial grammars.

8. Samuels (1999) also takes Cosmides and Tooby to task for suggesting that modules are computational processors, in one characterization, and software programs, in another characterization in his "Evolutionary Psychology and the Massive Modularity Hypothesis." But I think this appearance of incoherence can be discharged if we apply the principle of charity properly. Cosmides and Tooby clearly defend the former characterization in most of their works. The latter characterization is an isolated instance where they "liken" modules to software programs. They do not intend to claim identity as the relationship here. Rather, the idea is that in some respects modules and programs are similar, or some properties are shared between modules and software programs. Samuels attempts, in my view, to make a mountain out of a molehill here. At best, what is revealed about Cosmides and Tooby is that they sometimes offer sloppy formulations or even exaggerated descriptions of their position. Their enthusiasm, I think, has a tendency to get in the way of strict, scholarly prose. This, to be sure, is a failure on their part but, perhaps, an understandable failure.

9. See, for instance, the discussion at the end of Cosmides and Tooby (1997) "Dissecting the Computational Architecture of Social Inference Mechanisms," where Tooby says: "We're not arguing that there are no general rules. We are just suggesting that psychologists should consider the hypothesis that a given performance is generated by domain-specific mechanisms on an equal basis with the hypothesis that it is generated by domain-general mechanisms, rather than either ruling it out a priori or accepting a lower standard of evidence for the domain-general hypothesis" (p. 159). It is interesting to note that when I presented the "grid" to Cosmides and Tooby in a paper I gave at the Center for Evolutionary Psychology on March 4, 2003, Cosmides immediately noted that Tooby had used a similar grid to present the options to his students for many years. They also noted that they think A, B, C, and D are nonempty, though they had argued explicitly only for instantiations of A and D in their work.

10. See, for instance, Samuels (1999) and Fodor (2000), for more on this point.

11. Cosmides tells me that it was difficult at that time to insert any comment about evolution at all into a psychology journal. Hence, it was a battle to include the footnote in question.

12. See the introduction and chapter 1 of Barkow, Cosmides, and Tooby's *The Adapted Mind* (1992), for what amounts to a manifesto concerning the proper methodology to

follow when doing evolutionary psychology and the errors of the standard social science model.

13. There are many excellent texts and anthologies available on this literature. For instance, see Nisbett and Ross (1980); Kahneman, Slovic, and Tversky (1982); Baron (1988); Piatelli-Palmarini (1994); Dawes (1988); Sutherland (1994).

Chapter 2

1. See van Fraassen's *The Scientific Image* (1980), Boyd's "Scientific Realism" (1979), Quine's "On What There Is" (1969b), and Kuhn's *The Structure of Scientific Revolutions* (1962), for more on these points.

2. Bonjour's book is *The Structure of Empirical Knowledge* (1989). For papers on the coherence account of justification and knowledge, including Kornblith's paper, see Bender's *The Current State of the Coherence Theory* (1989). It should be emphasized that Bonjour has since given up the coherence account and has become one of its most persistent critics in recent works.

3. See Cherniak's book, *Minimal Rationality* (1986), for more on the inferential limitations of humans. Also, see Stich's *The Fragmentation of Reason* (1990), for a discussion of these and other empirical results.

Chapter 3

1. Quine describes this case in chapter 2 of *Word and Object* (1960).

2. For more on the principle of rationality, see Dennett's *The Intentional Stance* (1987) and Davidson's *Essays on Truth and Interpretation* (1984).

3. I would like to thank Francis Egan and Jerry Fodor for this objection.

4. Fodor, in conversation, has indicated to me that he thinks Millikan's mistake is to build the intensional idiom into the representation consumer by talking about how the consumer "needs oxygen-free water." Her response fails to naturalize the intensional idiom. In effect, she simply moves the problem from the representation-producer to the representation-consumer without resolving the issue.

5. Error is not the rule either, as Kornblith makes clear in his 1993 book, *Induction: Its Natural Ground*. In that book he notes that psychologists study abnormal visual and reasoning situations (or errors) as a means to understand the more typical cases where things go well.

6. For an alternative account, see Samuels, Stich, and Tremoulet (1998), "Rethinking Rationality: From Bleak Implications to Darwinian Modules."

7. See Samuels, Stich, and Tremoulet (1998), for more on this matter.

8. The central contrast concerning accounts of function is that between forward-looking, Cummins-style accounts and backward-looking, etiological, Wright-style accounts. Godfrey-Smith suggests, in *Complexity and the Function of Mind in Nature,* that one does not have to choose between these accounts (Godfrey-Smith 1996, p. 15). I do not share that view but I cannot argue for this point here.

9. I argued directly for this point in my (1996b), "Darwinian Algorithms and Indexical Representation."

10. For more on this point, see chapter 3, section 1.

11. I owe this clarification of Fodor's view to William Lycan.

12. I think a crucial factor concerning whether natural selection can slice matters as finely as propositional attitudes depends on there being empirical implications with respect to the propositional attitudes in question. For instance, if there is a cost/benefit structure to the relevant propositional attitudes, then the chances that those attitudes can be reconstructed by appeal to natural selection is a genuine possibility. If it were the case that there were no empirical implications concerning the attitudes, then—of course—it would be futile to attempt to reconstruct them by appeal to natural selection. But the point of my analysis is to show that there are such empirical implications.

Chapter 4

1. See Sober's *The Nature of Selection* (1984) for a useful discussion on this and related points. But see also G. C. Williams's (1966) classic, *Adaptation and Natural Selection,* perhaps the most influential book on evolutionary thinking in the last half century.

2. See my "Epistemic Norms and Evolutionary Success" (1990) and Dretske's "The Need To Know" (1989) for more on these points.

3. For insightful discussion on this topic see Lewontin's "The Evolution of Cognition" (1990) and Sober's "The Evolution of Rationality" (1981). But see also H. Plotkin's *Evolution in Mind* for worries about how we might look for such data and the difficulties involved. Barkow, Cosmides, and Tooby suggest a variety of strategies for such work in the introduction and chapter 1 of *The Adapted Mind* (1992).

4. See Cosmides (1989) and Cosmides and Tooby (1987), (1989), and (1992) for a detailed empirical and conceptual defense of the idea that humans satisfy deductive standards of reasoning where a social contract is involved in Wason selection tasks. See Cosmides and Tooby (1996) for the claim that humans engage in good inductive inference if problems are presented as frequencies, rather than single-case probabilities, in cases involving the conjunction, overconfidence, and the base-rate fallacy.

5. Stich's discussion of optimality ignores Goldman's (1986) claim in *Epistemology and Cognition* that speed and power vie with reliability as epistemic parameters. Contra Stich, no reliabilist would claim that only reliability matters.

6. Free riders can also be produced as a result of gene linkage where a neutral gene and an advantageous gene may be close together on one chromosome. Selection for one may increase the frequency of both genes (Sober 1984, p. 101).

7. See note 13 in chapter 1 for a list of such texts and anthologies.

8. The fact that the higher primates display protoreasoning adds weight to the suggestion that a primitive reasoning capacity was selected for among *Homo sapiens.* Gillan has documented what appears to be analogical reasoning among chimpanzees, and Premack has noted that chimpanzees seem to appreciate the concept of conservation. Michael Ruse has cataloged a great deal of evidence along these lines in his *Taking Darwin Seriously* (1986). We also find similar senses of logic and mathematics across cultures, which suggests biological roots. See, for instance, Ruse's discussion of Staal and Bockenski. On the negative side, John Anderson provides evidence of deductive inference failures in his *Cognitive Psychology and Its Implications* (1985), chapter 10.

9. See Harman's *Thought* (1973) for discussion of the lottery paradox, and see Goldman's "What Is Justified Belief?" (1979), Feldman's "Reliability and Justification" (1985), and Conee and Feldman's "The Generality Problem for Reliabilism" (1998), for more on the generality problem. Finally, see Barry Stroud's *The Significance of Philosophical Scepticism* (1984) for more on why skepticism is a problem for externalists. But also see Michael Williams's *Unnatural Doubts: Epistemological Realism and the Basis of Scepticism* (1991) for a skeptical update. Here are some more specific details. The lottery paradox is a problem for Goldman's reliabilism because the probability that one holds a losing ticket in a fair lottery is very high, suggesting that one might know that one is going to lose. Yet, someone has to win the lottery. The reliable process account of justification seems to sanction such beliefs because they are the result of a reliable process, i.e., good inductive reasoning. Yet it also seems clear that such beliefs are not justified enough for knowledge because someone will win the lottery. Hence, Goldman's account seems too weak. But see my discussion in section 4.4. For a description of the generality problem that confronts the reliable process account of justification, see section 3.8 and 4.4. Stroud's problem with externalism is that it does not make possible witting knowledge, i.e., knowledge that affords justification that is internally transparent to the cognizer. For this reason, Stroud thinks externalists fail to address skeptical concerns properly. Similar concerns with the internal transparency of justifiedness have been noted in various ways by internalists for the last twenty years or so. Bonjour's concern with being epistemically responsible is one example of this worry. Fumerton and Feldman are well known for voicing similar worries. (See section 5.1 for more on Fumerton and Stroud.)

10. Dretske (1971), Goldman (1986), and I (1986b) have all defended this view.

11. There is a substantial literature on the lottery paradox that begins with Harman's book, *Thought*. The specification of the width of a process type or the generality problem is addressed in Goldman's "What Is Justified Belief?" (1979) and developed by Richard Feldman in "Reliability and Justification" (1985).

12. I want to thank George Pappas for bringing this problem to my attention.

13. See John Pollock's "Epistemic Norms" (1987) for criticism of Goldman suggesting that there is no reason to think that reliability is a property of our cognitive processes. Goldman does connect the notion of true belief with genetic fitness in his *Epistemology and Cognition* (1986), p. 98. My claim is that he needs to say much more about the nature of these connections if this story is to be made plausible.

14. Students often feel like this when dealing with faculty members at graduate school!

15. There are accounts of belief that deny that belief presupposes language. Robert Stalnaker, for instance, has defended one such view in his (1984).

Chapter 5

1. See, for instance, Richard Fumerton's "Scepticism and Naturalistic Epistemology" (pp. 321–340) and Mark Kaplan's "Epistemology Denatured" (pp. 350–365), both in French, Uehling, and Wettstein (1994). But also see Barry Stroud's *The Significance of Philosophical Scepticism* (1984), chapter 6, and "Understanding Human Knowledge in General" in Clay and Lehrer (1989), and Mark Kaplan's "Epistemology on Holiday" (1991). See also Bonjour's *The Structure of Empirical Knowledge* (1986).

2. Here I have in mind an attitude that, I think, lots of philosophers of science share. One can find the sentiment expressed in the preface and introduction to Stich's *The Fragmentation of Reason* (1990) and in Nozick's introduction to *Philosophical Explanations* (1981), though I do not think of either author primarily as a philosopher of science. It is more typical of philosophers of science to simply dismiss analytic epistemology, rather than write about it.

3. This distinction is similar, but not identical, to Goldman's distinction between *ex ante* and *ex post* justifiedness in "What Is Justified Belief?" (1979) and his distinction between regulative and nonregulative justifiedness in "The Internalist Conception of Knowledge" (1980). It also has an ancestor in my distinction between objective and subjective justifiedness in "Reliability and Two Kinds of Justified Belief" (1986b) and Goldman's strong versus weak distinction in his "Strong and Weak Justification" (1992). Kitcher has, of course, used the term "meliorative" in the way I do in his "The Naturalists Return" (1992).

4. See Carnap's "Truth and Confirmation" (1949) in Herbert Feigl and Wilfred Sellars (eds.), *Readings in Philosophical Analysis.*

5. Henry Kyburg (in conversation), for instance, denies that empirical psychology and evolutionary biology bear any relevance to his concerns. He even goes so far as to deny that evolutionary theory has any bearing on any philosophical issues. It is safe to conclude, I think, that he is a nonnaturalist.

6. Of course, I will take up exactly this strategy in chapter 5.

7. See Harvey Siegel, "Justification, Discovery, and the Naturalizing of Epistemology" (1980), "Empirical Psychology, Naturalized Epistemology and First Philosophy" (1984a), "What Is the Question Concerning the Rationality of Science?" (1984b), and "Philosophy of Science Naturalized? Some Problems with Giere's Naturalism" (1989).

8. See Larry Laudan's "Normative Naturalism" (1989), and Ronald Giere's *Explaining Science: A Cognitive Approach* (1988).

9. For more on Bayesian inference, see William Harper, *Ifs: Conditionals, Belief, Chance, and Time* (1980), in *The Western Ontario Series in Philosophy of Science*.

10. In conversation (March 4, 2003), Cosmides tells me that the notion of cheater detection was actually in her Harvard dissertation back in 1986. Also, see Cosmides and Tooby (1989, p. 84) for further evidence supporting her claim.

11. However, there is a problem with Cummins's evidence in that it has not be replicated to date. In particular, an attempt by researchers at Cosmides and Tooby's Center for Evolutionary Psychology at the University of California, Santa Barbara failed to replicate Cummins's results.

Chapter 6

1. Feldman's article is "Rationality, Reliability, and Natural Selection" in *Philosophy of Science* (1988), and Fumerton's article is "Scepticism and Naturalistic Epistemology," in French, Uehling, and Wettstein (1994).

2. See Goldman's "Folk Psychology and Scientific Epistemology" in *Liaisons* (1992). Kornblith argues for this view in "Knowledge in Humans and Other Animals" (1999). Papineau made this suggestion in a presentation at Rutgers at the Cognitive Basis of Science Conference on November 1, 1999.

3. Goldman, for instance, takes this position in "What Is Justified Belief?" (1979).

4. One might think that knowledge is not a kind of any sort because it is a Wittgensteinian game. According to Wittgenstein, such a game is not a mystery at all despite the fact that we cannot give an analysis of it. There may be merit to this proposal. I will leave it to the reader to think about this possibility. I thank George Pappas for bringing this possibility to my attention.

5. See Devitt's "The Methodology of Naturalistic Semantics" (1994), Millikan's "Naturalist Reflections on Knowledge," reprinted in her (1993), pp. 241–264, and Stich's "Naturalizing Epistemology: Quine, Simon, and the Prospects for Pragmatism" (1993). See also, Kornblith (2002).

6. For more details on module reliability, see chapter 2, section 8.

7. I owe this suggestion to Hilary Kornblith.

Chapter 7

1. See Quine's *The Pursuit of Truth* (1992), p. 18, and his *Epistemology Naturalizing* (1969) for more on his sense of the normative in epistemology. Richard Foley's "Quine and Naturalized Epistemology," in French, Uehling, and Wettstein (1994), pp. 243–261, is the best study of Quine's position on the normative in my view. See Goldman, *Epistemology and Cognition* (1986), chapter 3, and "What Is Justified Belief?" (1979) for his view of the normative in epistemology. Stich's view on the normative can be found in his "Naturalizing Epistemology: Quine, Simon and the Prospects for Pragmatism" (1993).

2. Kornblith has rescinded this interpretation of Quine in conversation, but he did not alter his position in print.

3. See Ruse's *Taking Darwin Seriously: A Naturalistic Approach to Philosophy* (1986) for more on this point. The idea is that there is a consensus about the fact of evolution even though it is true that there is serious debate about the units of selection and the rate of change.

References

Adams, F., and Clarke, M. (2003). "Toward Saving Nozick from Kripke." In W. Loffler and P. Weingartner, eds., *Proceedings of the Twenty-Sixth International Wittgenstein Symposium*, pp. 18–19. Kirchberg: The Austrian Wittgenstein Society.

Anderson, J. (1985). *Cognitive Psychology and Its Implications*, second edition. New York: W. H. Freeman.

Baillargeon, R. R. (1987). "Young Infants Reasoning about the Physical and Spatial Properties of a Hidden Object." *Cognitive Development* 2: 170–200.

Barkow, J., Cosmides, L., and Tooby, J., eds. (1992). *The Adapted Mind: Evolutionary Psychology and the Generation of Culture*. New York: Oxford University Press.

Baron, J. (1988). *Thinking and Deciding*. Cambridge: Cambridge University Press.

Baron-Cohen, S. (1995). *Mindblindness: An Essay on Autism and Theory of Mind*. Cambridge, Mass.: The MIT Press.

Bechtel, W. (1992). *Connectionism and the Mind: An Introduction to Parallel Processing Networks*. Oxford: Blackwell.

Bender, J., ed. (1989). *The Current State of the Coherence Theory*. Dordrecht: Kluwer Academic.

Bogdan, R., ed. (1986). *Belief*. Oxford: Oxford University Press.

Bonjour, L. (1986). *The Structure of Empirical Knowledge*. Cambridge, Mass.: Harvard University Press.

Boyd, R. (1979). "Scientific Realism." In Boyd, Gasper, and Trout (1990).

Boyd, R., Gasper, P., and Trout, J. D., eds. (1990). *The Philosophy of Science*. Cambridge, Mass.: The MIT Press.

Braine, M. D. S. (1978). "On the Relationship between the Natural Logic of Reasoning and Standard Logic." *Psychological Review* 85: 1–21.

Braine, M. D. S., and O'Brien, D. P. (1991). "A Theory of If: Lexical Entry, Reasoning Program, and Pragmatic Principles." *Psychological Review* 98: 182–203.

Braine, M. D. S., Reiser, B. J., and Rumain, B. (1984). "Some Empirical Justification for a Theory of Natural Propositional Logic." In *The Psychology of Learning and Motivation,* volume 18, pp. 313–371. New York: Academic Press.

Brase, L., Cosmides, L., and Tooby, J. (1998). "Individuation, Counting, and Statistical Inference: The Role of Frequency and Whole-Object Representations in Judgement under Uncertainty." *Journal of Experimental Psychology* (general) 127: 3–21.

Carey, S., and Gelman, R. (1991). *Epigenesis of the Mind: Essays in Biology and Knowledge.* Hillsdale, N.J.: Lawrence Erlbaum.

Carey, S., and Spelke, E. (1994). "Domain-specific Knowledge and Conceptual Change." In Hirshfield and Gelman (1994).

Carnap, R. (1938). "Logical Foundations of the Unity of Science." In *Encyclopedia of Unified Science.* Chicago, Ill.: University of Chicago Press.

——— (1949). "Truth and Confirmation." In Feigl and Sellars (1949).

Carruthers, P., and Smith, P., eds. (1996). *Theories of Theories of Mind.* Cambridge: Cambridge University Press.

Cheng, P. (1986). "A Purely Geometric Module in the Rat's Spatial Representation." *Cognition* 23: 149–178.

Cheng, P., and Gallistel, C. R. (1984). "Testing the Geometric Power of an Animal's Spatial Representation." In H. L. Roitblat, T. G. Bever, and H. S. Terrace, eds., *Animal Cognition,* pp. 409–423. Hillsdale, N.J: Lawrence Erlbaum.

Cheng, P., and Holyoak, K. (1985). "Pragmatic Reasoning Schemas." *Cognitive Psychology* 17: 391–416.

——— (1989). "On the Natural Selection of Reasoning Theories." *Cognition* 33: 285–313.

Cheng, P., Holyoak, K., Nisbett, R., and Oliver, L. (1986). "Pragmatic Reasoning versus Syntactic Approaches to Training Deductive Reasoning." *Cognitive Psychology* 18: 293–328.

Cherniak, C. (1986). *Minimal Rationality.* Cambridge, Mass.: The MIT Press.

Chomsky, N. (1980). *Rules and Representations.* New York: Columbia University Press.

Churchland, P. (1989). *A Neurocomputational Perspective: The Nature of Mind and the Structure of Science.* Cambridge, Mass.: The MIT Press.

Clark, A. (1993). *Associative Engines: Connectionism, Concepts, and Representational Change.* Cambridge, Mass.: The MIT Press.

Clarke, M. (1986a). "Doxastic Voluntarism and Forced Belief." *Philosophical Studies* 50: 39–51.

—— (1986b). "Reliability and Two Kinds of Epistemic Justification." In N. Garver and P. Hare, eds., *Naturalism and Rationality,* pp. 159–170. Buffalo, N.Y.: Prometheus Press.

—— (1990). "Epistemic Norms and Evolutionary Success." *Synthese* 85: 231–244.

—— (1996a). "Knowledge and Indexical Representation." In R. S. Cohen and M. Marion, eds., *Boston Studies in the Philosophy of Science,* volume 178, pp. 53–62. Amsterdam: Reidel.

—— (1996b). "Darwinian Algorithms and Indexical Representation." *Philosophy of Science* 63 (1): 27–47.

—— (2000). "Reliabilism and the Meliorative Project." In R. Cobb-Stevens, ed., *Proceedings of the Twentieth World Congress of Philosophy,* volume 5, pp. 75–82. Bowling Green, Ohio: Philosophy Documentation Center.

—— (2003). "The Mind almost Works That Way." In A. Burge, ed., *Proceedings of the Hawaii International Conference on Arts and Humanities.* Honolulu, Hawaii: University of Hawaii Press.

Clay, M., and Lehrer, K., eds. (1989). *Knowledge and Scepticism.* Boulder, Colo.: Westview.

Cohen, J. (1981). "Can Human Irrationality Be Experimentally Demonstrated?" *Behavioral and Brain Sciences* 4: 317–370.

—— (1986). *The Dialogue of Reason.* Oxford: Clarendon Press.

Conee, E., and Feldman, R. (1998). "The Generality Problem for Reliabilism." *Philosophical Studies* 89 (1): 1–29.

Cosmides, L. (1989). "The Logic of Social Exchange: Has Natural Selection Shaped How Humans Reason?" *Cognition* 31: 187–276.

Cosmides, L., and Tooby, J. (1987). "From Evolution to Behavior: Evolutionary Psychology as the Missing Link." In Dupre (1987).

—— (1989). "Evolutionary Psychology and the Generation of Culture, Part II. A Computational Theory of Social Exchange." *Ethology and Sociobiology* 10: 51–97.

—— (1992). "Cognitive Adaptations for Social Exchange." In Barkow, Cosmides, and Tooby (1992).

—— (1994). "Origins of Domain-specificity: The Evolution of Functional Organization." In Hirschfield and Gelman (1994), pp. 85–116.

—— (1995). Foreword to Baron-Cohen (1995).

—————— (1996). "Are Humans Good Intuitive Statisticians After All? Rethinking Some Conclusions from the Literature on Judgement under Uncertainty." *Cognition* 58: 1–73.

—————— (1997a). "Dissecting the Computational Architecture of Social Inference Mechanisms." In the Ciba Foundation, ed., *Characterizing Human Psychological Adaptations,* pp. 132–159. New York: John Wiley.

—————— (1997b). "The Modular Nature of Human Intelligence." In Scheibel and Schopf (1997), pp. 71–101.

Cummins, D. D. (1996). "Evidence for the Innateness of Deontic Reasoning." *Mind and Language* 11 (2): 160–190.

Cummins, D. D., and Allen, C., eds. (1998). *The Evolution of Mind.* New York: Oxford University Press.

Damasio, A. R. (1994). *Descartes' Error: Emotions, Reason, and the Human Brain.* New York: G. P. Putnam.

Darwin, C. (1859). *The Origin of Species.* New York: New American Library.

Davidson, D. (1980). *Essays on Action and Events.* New York: Oxford University Press.

—————— (1984). *Essays on Truth and Interpretation.* New York: Oxford University Press.

Davies, M., and Stone, T., eds. (1996). *Mental Simulation: Philosophical and Psychological Essays.* Oxford: Blackwell.

Dawes, R. (1988). *Rational Choice in an Uncertain World.* Orlando, Fla.: Harcourt Brace Jovanovich.

Dennett, D. (1987). *The Intentional Stance.* Cambridge, Mass.: The MIT Press.

—————— (1992). *Consciousness Explained.* New York: Little, Brown.

Dennett, D., and Gould, S. J. (1997). "Darwinian Fundamentalism: An Exchange." *New York Review of Books,* August 14.

Devitt, M. (1994). "The Methodology of Naturalistic Semantics." *Journal of Philosophy* 91: 545–572.

Dretske, F. (1971). "Conclusive Reasons." *Australasian Journal of Philosophy* 49 (1): 1–22.

—————— (1980). *Knowledge and the Flow of Information.* Cambridge, Mass.: The MIT Press.

—————— (1986). "Misrepresentation." In Bogdan (1986), pp. 17–36.

—————— (1988). *Explaining Behavior: Reasons in a World of Causes.* Cambridge, Mass.: The MIT Press.

———— (1989). "The Need to Know." In Clay and Lehrer (1989), pp. 89–100.

———— (1990). "Does Meaning Matter?" In Villaneuva (1990), pp. 5–17.

Dupre, J., ed. (1987). *The Latest on the Best: Essays on Evolution and Optimality.* Cambridge, Mass.: The MIT Press.

Elman, J., Bates, E., Johnson, M., Karmiloff-Smith, A., Parisi, D., and Plunkett, K. (1996). *Rethinking Innateness: A Connectionist Perspective on Development.* Cambridge, Mass.: The MIT Press.

Evans, J. St. B. T. (1982). *The Psychology of Deductive Reasoning.* London: Routledge and Kegan Paul.

———— (1989). *Bias in Human Reasoning: Causes and Consequences.* London: Lawrence Erlbaum.

Evans, J. St. B. T., Newstead, S. E., and Byrne, R. M. J. (1993). *Human Reasoning.* Hove: Lawrence Erlbaum.

Feigl, H., and Sellars, W., eds. (1949). *Readings in Philosophical Analysis.* New York: Appleton-Century-Crofts.

Feldman, R. (1985). "Reliability and Justification." *Monist* 63 (1): 159–174.

———— (1988). "Rationality, Reliability, and Natural Selection." *Philosophy of Science* 55: 1–20.

Fiddick, L., Cosmides, L., and Tooby, J. (2000). "No Interpretation without Representation: The Role of Domain-specific Representations and Inferences in the Wason Selection Task." *Cognition* 77: 1–79.

Fieldler, K. (1988). "The Dependence of the Conjunction Fallacy on Subtle Linguistic Factors." *Psychological Research* 50: 123–129.

Fodor, J. (1975). *The Language of Thought.* Cambridge, Mass.: The MIT Press.

———— (1983). *The Modularity of Mind.* Cambridge, Mass.: The MIT Press.

———— (1990). "Psychosemantics." In Lycan (1990).

———— (1987). *Psychosemantics.* Cambridge, Mass.: The MIT Press.

———— (1990). *A Theory of Content and Other Essays.* Cambridge, Mass.: The MIT Press.

———— (1990). "Reply to Dretske's 'Does Meaning Matter?'" In Villaneuva (1990), pp. 28–35.

———— (1994). *The Elm and the Expert: Mentalese and Its Semantics.* Cambridge, Mass.: The MIT Press.

———— (1998). *In Critical Condition: Polemical Essays on Cognitive Science and the Philosophy of Mind.* Cambridge, Mass.: The MIT Press.

—— (2000). *The Mind Doesn't Work That Way.* Cambridge, Mass.: The MIT Press.

Fodor, J., and LePore, E. (1992). *Holism: A Shopper's Guide.* Cambridge, Mass.: The MIT Press.

Foley, R. (1994). "Quine and Naturalized Epistemology." In French, Uehling, and Wettstein (1994), pp. 243–261.

French, P., Uehling, T., Jr., and Wettstein, H., eds. (1977). *Midwest Studies in Philosophy: Philosophy of Language,* volume 2. Minneapolis, Minn.: University of Minnesota Press.

—— (1980). *Midwest Studies in Philosophy: Studies in Epistemology,* volume 5. Minneapolis, Minn.: University of Minnesota Press.

—— (1994). *Midwest Studies in Philosophy: Philosophical Naturalism,* volume 19. Minneapolis, Minn.: University of Minnesota Press.

Freyd, J. J. (1987). "Dynamic Mental Representations." *Psychological Review* 94: 427–438.

Fumerton, R. (1994). "Scepticism and Naturalistic Epistemology." In French, Uehling, and Wettstein (1994), pp. 321–340.

Gallistel, C. R. (1990). *The Organization of Learning.* Cambridge, Mass.: The MIT Press.

Gallistel, C. R., and Gelman, R. (1992). "Verbal and Preverbal Counting and Computation." *Cognition* 44: 43–74.

Giere, R. (1985). "Philosophy of Science Naturalized." *Philosophy of Science* 52: 331–356.

—— (1988). *Explaining Science: A Cognitive Approach.* Chicago, Ill.: University of Chicago Press.

Gigerenzer, G. (1991). "How to Make Cognitive Illusions Disappear: Beyond Heuristics and Biases." *European Review of Social Psychology* 2: 83–115.

Gigerenzer, G., and Hoffrage, U. (1995). "How to Improve Bayesian Reasoning without Instruction: Frequency Formats." *Psychological Review* 102: 684–704.

Gigerenzer, G., Hoffrage, U., and Kleinbolting, H. (1991). "Probabilistic Mental Models: A Brunswickean Theory of Confidence." *Psychological Review* 98: 506–528.

Gigerenzer, G., and Hug, K. (1992). "Domain-specific Reasoning: Social Contracts, Cheating and Perspective Change." *Cognition* 43: 127–171.

Gigerenzer, G., and Murray, D. (1987). *Cognition as Intuitive Statistics.* Hillsdale, N.J.: Lawrence Erlbaum.

Godfrey-Smith, P. (1996). *Complexity and the Function of Mind in Nature.* Cambridge: Cambridge University Press.

Goldman, A. (1967). "A Causal Theory of Knowledge." *Journal of Philosophy* 64: 357–372.

———— (1979). "What Is Justified Belief?" In G. S. Pappas, ed., *Justification and Knowledge*. Amsterdam: Kluwer Academic.

———— (1980). "The Internalist Conception of Justification." In French, Uehling, and Wettstein (1980).

———— (1986). *Epistemology and Cognition*. Cambridge, Mass.: Harvard University Press.

———— (1989). "Interpretation Psychologized." *Mind and Language* 4: 161–185.

———— (1992a). "Epistemic Folkways and Scientific Epistemology." In his (1992b), pp. 155–175.

———— (1992b). *Liaisons: Philosophy Meets the Cognitive and Social Sciences*. Cambridge, Mass.: The MIT Press.

———— (1992c). "Strong and Weak Justification." In his (1992b), pp. 127–142.

Gould, S. J. (1992). "The Confusion over Evolution." *New York Review of Books,* November 19.

———— (1997a). "Darwinian Fundamentalism," part 1. *New York Review of Books,* June 12.

———— (1997b). "Evolution: The Pleasures of Pluralism," part 2. *New York Review of Books,* June 26.

Gould, S. J., and Lewontin, R. (1979). "The Spandrels of San Marco and the Panglossian Paradigm: A Critique of the Adaptationist Program." *Proceedings of the Royal Society* B205: 581–98.

Guttenplan, S., ed. (1994). *A Companion to the Philosophy of Mind*. Oxford: Blackwell.

Harman, G. (1973). *Thought*. Princeton, N.J.: Princeton University Press.

Harper, W., Pierce, G., and Stalnaker, R., eds. (1980). *Ifs: Conditionals, Belief, Chance, and Time. The Western Ontario Series in Philosophy of Science,* volume 15. Dordrecht: Kluwer Academic.

Hermer, L., and Spelke, E. (1996). "Modularity and Development: The Case of Spatial Reorientation." *Cognition* 61: 195–232.

Hirshfield, L., and Gelman, S., eds. (1994). *Mapping the Mind: Domain-specificity in Cognition and Culture*. Cambridge: Cambridge University Press.

Hookway, C., and Peterson, D., eds. (1993). *Philosophy and Cognitive Science* (Royal Institute of Philosophy Supplement 34). Cambridge: Cambridge University Press.

Jackendoff, R. (1992). *Languages of the Mind*. Cambridge: Cambridge University Press.

Jerison, H. (1973). *The Evolution of the Brain and Intelligence*. New York: Academic Press.

Johnson, M., and Morton, J. (1991). *Biology and Cognitive Development: The Case of Face Recognition*. London: Blackwell.

Johnson-Laird, P. N. (1983). *Mental Models*. Cambridge, Mass.: Harvard University Press.

Kahneman, D., Slovic, P., and Tversky, A., eds. (1982). *Judgement under Uncertainty: Heuristics and Biases*. Cambridge: Cambridge University Press.

Kaplan, M. (1985). "It's Not What You Know That Counts." *Journal of Philosophy* 82: 350–363.

——— (1991). "Epistemology on Holiday." *Journal of Philosophy* 88: 132–154.

——— (1994). "Epistemology Denatured." In French, Uehling, and Wettstein (1994), pp. 350–365.

Karmiloff-Smith, A. (1992), *Beyond Modularity: A Developmental Perspective on Cognitive Science*. Cambridge, Mass.: The MIT Press.

Kitcher, P. (1992). "The Naturalists Return." *Philosophical Review* 101: 53–114.

Kornblith, H. (1985). *Naturalizing Epistemology*. Cambridge, Mass.: The MIT Press.

——— (1993). *Induction: Its Natural Ground*. Cambridge, Mass.: The MIT Press.

——— (1994). "The Epistemology of Science and the Epistemology of Everyday Life." Unpublished lecture delivered at the Rutgers/Princeton epistemology conference.

——— (1999). "Knowledge in Humans and Other Animals." *Philosophical Perspectives* 13: 327–346.

——— (2002). *Knowledge and Its Place in Nature*. Oxford: Oxford University Press.

Kuhn, T. (1962). *The Structure of Scientific Revolutions*. Chicago, Ill.: University of Chicago Press.

Kyberg, H. (1961). *Probability and the Logic of Rational Belief*. Middletown, Ohio: Wesleyan University Press.

Laudan, L. (1987). "Progress or Rationality? The Prospects for Normative Naturalism." *American Philosophical Quarterly* 24 (1): 19–31.

——— (1990). "Normative Naturalism." *Philosophy of Science* 57: 44–59.

LePore, E., and Pylyshyn, Z., eds. (1998). *Rutgers Invitation to Cognitive Science*. Oxford: Blackwell.

Leslie, A. (1984). "Infant Perception of a Manual Pick-Up Event." *British Journal of Developmental Psychology* 2: 19–32.

—— (1994). "ToMM, ToBY, and Agency: Core Architecture and Domain Specificity." In Hirshfeld and Gelman (1994), pp. 119–148.

Lewontin, R. (1990). "The Evolution of Cognition." In Osherson and Smith (1990), pp. 229–246.

Lycan, William G., ed. (1990). *Mind and Cognition.* Oxford: Blackwell.

Manktelow, K. I., and Over, D. E. (1990). *Inference and Understanding.* London: Routledge.

—— (1991). "Social Roles and Utilities in Reasoning with Deontic Conditionals." *Cognition* 39: 85–105.

—— (1995). "Deontic Reasoning." In S. E. Newstead and J. St. B. T. Evans, eds., *Perspectives on Thinking and Reasoning.* Hillsdale, N.J.: Lawrence Erlbaum.

Marion, M., and Cohen, R. S., eds. (1996). *Boston Studies in the Philosophy of Science,* volume 178. Amsterdam: Reidel.

Marks, I. M. (1977). *Fears, Phobias, and Rituals.* New York: Oxford University Press.

Marr, D. (1982). *Vision: A Computational Investigation into the Human Representation and Processing of Visual Information.* San Francisco, Calif.: Freeman.

McCauley, C., and Stitt, C. L. (1978). "An Individual and Quantitative Measure of Stereotypes." *Journal of Personality and Social Psychology* 36: 929–940.

McGinn, C. (1992). "Logic, Mind, and Mathematics." In B. Dahlboom, ed., *Dennett and His Critics.* Cambridge: Blackwell.

Millikan, R. (1993). *White Queen Psychology and Other Essays for Alice.* Cambridge, Mass.: The MIT Press.

Nisbett, R. and Ross, L., eds. (1980). *Human Inference: Strategies and Shortcomings of Social Judgement.* Englewood Cliffs, N.J.: Prentice-Hall.

Nozick, R. (1981). *Philosophical Explanations.* Cambridge, Mass.: Harvard University Press.

—— (1993). *The Nature of Rationality.* Cambridge, Mass.: Harvard University Press.

Oaksford, M., and Chater, N. (1994). "A Rational Analysis of the Selection Task as Optimal Data Selection." *Psychological Review* 101: 608–631.

—— (1998). *Rationality in an Uncertain World.* East Sussex: Psychology Press.

Osherson, D. (1975). "Logic and Models of Logical Thinking." In R. J. Falmagne, ed., *Reasoning: Representation and Process.* Hillsdale, N.J.: Lawrence Erlbaum.

Osherson, D., and Smith, E. (1990). *Thinking: An Invitation to Cognitive Science.* Cambridge, Mass.: The MIT Press.

Piatelli-Palmarini, M. (1994). *Inevitable Illusions: How Mistakes of Reason Rule Our Minds*. New York: John Wiley.

Pinker, S. (1994). *The Language Instinct*. New York: William Morrow.

—— (1997). *How the Mind Works*. New York: W. W. Norton.

—— (2002). *The Blank Slate: The Modern Denial of Human Nature*. New York: Viking Press.

Pinker, S., and Bloom, P. (1990). "Natural Language and Natural Selection." *Behavioral and Brain Science* 13: 707–784.

Pinker, S., and Gould, S. J. (1997). "Evolutionary Psychology: An Exchange." *New York Review of Books,* October 9.

Plato (1961). "Meno." In Hamilton and Cairns, eds., *Plato: The Collected Dialogues*. Princeton, N.J.: Princeton University Press.

Plotkin, H. (1997). *Evolution in Mind*. London: Alan Lane.

Pollock, J. (1987). "Epistemic Norms." *Synthese* 71: 61–95.

Quine, W. V. O. (1960). *Word and Object*. Cambridge, Mass.: The MIT Press.

—— (1969a). *Ontological Relativity and Other Essays*. New York: Columbia University Press.

—— (1969b). "On What There Is." In his (1969a).

—— (1969c). "Epistemology Naturalized." In his (1969a), pp.69–90.

—— (1992). *Pursuit of Truth*. Cambridge, Mass.: Harvard University Press.

Ramachandran, U. S. (1990). "Visual Perception in People and Machines." In A. Blake and T. Troscianko, eds., *AI and the Eye*. New York: John Wiley.

Reber, P. J., and Squire, L. R. (1999). "Intact Learning of Artificial Grammars and Intact Category Learning by Patients with Parkinson's Disease." *Behavioral Neuroscience* 113: 235–242.

Ridley, M. (1993). *Evolution*. New York: Blackwell Scientific.

Rips, L. J. (1983). "Cognitive Processes in Propositional Reasoning." *Psychological Review* 90: 38–71.

—— (1994). *The Psychology of Proof*. Cambridge, Mass.: The MIT Press.

Rode, C., Cosmides, L., Hell, W., and Tooby, J. (1999). "When and Why Do People Avoid Unknown Probabilities in Decisions under Uncertainty? Testing Some Predictions from Optimal Foraging Theory." *Cognition* 72: 269–304.

Rosch, E. (1978). "Principles of Categorization." In Rosch and Lloyd (1978).

Rosch, E., and Lloyd, B. B., eds. (1978). *Cognition and Categorization.* Hillsdale, N.J.: Lawrence Erlbaum.

Rumain, B., Connell, J., and Braine, M. D. S. (1983). "Conversational Comprehension Processes Are Responsible for Reasoning Fallacies in Children as Well as Adults: IF Is Not the Biconditional." *Developmental Psychology* 19: 471–481.

Ruse, M. (1986). *Taking Darwin Seriously: A Naturalistic Approach to Philosophy.* Oxford: Blackwell.

Russell, B., and Whitehead, A. (1905). *Principia Mathematica.* Oxford: Oxford University Press.

Samuels, R. (1998). "Evolutionary Psychology and the Massive Modularity Hypothesis." *British Journal for the Philosophy of Science* 49: 575–602.

Samuels, R., Stich, S., and Tremoulet, P. (1998). "Rethinking Rationality: From Bleak Implications to Darwinian Modules." In LePore and Pylyshyn (1998), pp. 130–160.

Sartwell, C. (1992). "Why Knowledge Is Merely True Belief." *Journal of Philosophy* 89 (4): 167–180.

Scheibel, A., and Schopf, J. W., eds. (1997). *The Origin and Evolution of Intelligence.* Sudbury, Mass.: Jones and Bartlett.

Segal, G. (1996). "The Modularity of Theory of Mind." In Carruthers and Smith (1996), pp. 141–157.

Shannon, C. and Weaver, W. (1949). *The Mathematical Theory of Communication.* Champaign, Ill.: University of Illinois Press.

Shepard, R. N. (1984). "Ecological Constraints on Internal Representation: Resonant Kinematics of Perceiving, Imagining, Thinking, and Dreaming." *Psychological Review* 91: 417–447.

Shiffrar, M., and Freyd, J. J. (1990). "Apparent Motion of the Human Body." *Psychological Science* 71: 257–264.

Siegel, H. (1980). "Justification, Discovery, and the Naturalizing of Epistemology." *Philosophy of Science* 47 (2): 297–321.

——— (1984a). "Empirical Psychology, Naturalized Epistemology, and First Philosophy." *Philosophy of Science* 51 (4): 667–676.

——— (1984b). "What Is the Question Concerning the Rationality of Science?" *Philosophy of Science* 52 (4): 517–537.

——— (1989). "Philosophy of Science Naturalized? Some Problems with Giere's Naturalism." *Studies in History and Philosophy of Science* 20 (3): 365–375.

Sober, E. (1981). "The Evolution of Rationality." *Synthese* 46: 95–120.

—— (1984). *The Nature of Selection.* Cambridge, Mass.: The MIT Press.

Spelke, E. (1988). "Where Perceiving Ends and Thinking Begins: The Apprehension of Objects in Infancy." In A. Yonas, ed., *Perceptual Development in Infancy. Minnesota Symposium on Child Psychology,* volume 20, pp. 191–234. Hillsdale, N.J.: Lawrence Erlbaum.

—— (1990). "Principles of Object Perception." *Cognitive Science* 14: 29–56.

—— (1991). "Physical Knowledge in Infancy: Reflections on Piaget's Theory." In Carey and Gelman (1991).

Sperber, D. (1994). "The Modularity of Thought and the Epidemiology of Representations." In Hirschfield and Gelman (1994), pp. 39–67.

Sperber, D., Cara, F., and Girotto, V. (1995). "Relevance Theory Explains the Selection Task." *Cognition* 57: 31–95.

Sperber, D., and Wilson, D. (1986). *Relevance: Communication and Cognition.* Oxford: Blackwell.

Stalnaker, R. (1984). *Inquiry.* Cambridge, Mass.: The MIT Press.

Stampe, D. (1977). "Toward a Causal Theory of Linguistic Representation." In French, Uehling, and Wettstein (1997), pp. 99–115.

Stein, E. (1996). *Without Good Reason.* Oxford: Clarendon Press.

Stich, S. (1983). *From Folk Psychology to Cognitive Science.* Cambridge, Mass.: The MIT Press.

—— (1990). *The Fragmentation of Reason.* Cambridge, Mass.: The MIT Press.

—— (1993). "Naturalizing Epistemology: Quine, Simon, and the Prospects for Pragmatism." In Hookway and Peterson (1993), pp. 1–18.

Stroud, B. (1984). *The Significance of Philosophical Scepticism.* Oxford: Oxford University Press.

—— (1989). "Understanding Human Knowledge in General." In Clay and Lehrer (1989), pp. 31–50.

Sutherland, S. (1994). *Irrationality: Why We Don't Think Straight!* New Brunswick, N.J.: Rutgers University Press.

Tooby, J., and Cosmides, L. (1989). "Evolutionary Psychology and the Generation of Culture, Part I. Theoretical Considerations." *Ethology and Sociobiology* 10: 29–49.

—— (1990). "On the Universality of Human Nature and the Uniqueness of the Individual: The Role of Genetics and Adaptation." *Journal of Personality* 58 (1): 17–67.

—— (1992). "The Psychological Foundations of Culture." In Barkow, Cosmides, and Tooby (1992), pp. 19–136.

———— (1996). "Friendship and the Banker's Paradox: Other Pathways to the Evolution of Adaptations for Altruism." *Proceedings of the British Academy* 88: 119–143.

———— (1997). Letter to the Editor of the *New York Review of Books* on S. J. Gould's "Darwinian Fundamentalism" (June 12, 1997) and "Evolution: The Pleasures of Pluralism" (June 26, 1997). *New York Review of Books,* July 9.

van Fraassen, B. (1980). *The Scientific Image.* Oxford: Oxford University Press.

Villaneuva, E., ed. (1990). *Information, Semantics, and Epistemology.* Cambridge: Blackwell.

Wason, P. C. (1968). "Reasoning about a Rule." *Quarterly Journal of Experimental Psychology* 20: 273–281.

Wason, P. C., and Johnson-Laird, P. N. (1972). *Psychology of Reasoning: Structure and Content.* Cambridge, Mass.: Harvard University Press.

Weaver, W. (1949). "Recent Contributions to the Mathematical Theory of Communication." In Shannon and Weaver (1949).

Wiener, N. (1948). *Cybernetics.* New York: John Wiley.

Williams, G. C. (1966). *Adaptation and Natural Selection.* Princeton, N.J.: Princeton University Press.

Williams, M. (1991). *Unnatural Doubts: Epistemological Realism and the Basis of Scepticism.* Oxford: Blackwell.

Wright, L. (1998). "Functions." In M. Bekoff and G. Lauder, eds., *Nature's Purposes: Analyses of Function and Design in Biology.* Cambridge, Mass.: The MIT Press.

Index

Abductive inference, 19, 30–42
Adapticism, 115, 119–120, 126, 128, 129, 152–153
Allen, C., 121
Anderson, J., 159n8
Aristotle, 152
Associationism. *See* Reasoning theories, availability
Austin, J. L., 132

Barkow, J., 2, 4, 155n5, 156n9, 159n10
Barnes, B., 86
Baron, J., 157n13
Base-rate, neglect of, 10, 12, 115, 118–119, 158n4
Bayes's theorem, 126–127, 161n9
Bechtel, W., 13
Bloor, D., 86
Bonjour, L., 32–33, 157ch2n2, 160n1
Boyd, R., 136–137
Braine, M., 122
Burne, R. M. J., 120

Cara, F., 123–125
Carey, S., 28, 139
Carnap, R., 105, 107–109, 126–127, 160n4
Causal theory, of content and meaning, 14, 43–44
Chater, N., 123

Cheater detection module. *See* Reasoning theories, cheater detection
Cheng, P., 11, 39, 93, 96, 98, 117, 125
Cherniak, C., 33, 157ch2n3
Chomsky, N., 19–20, 54
Chomsky module. *See* Module, Chomsky
Clark, A., 13
Clarke, M., 81, 84, 158n9, 159n10
Competence/performance distinction, 54–56
Conee, E., 64, 85–86, 159n9
Conjunction fallacy, 10, 115–116, 118–119, 158n4
Cosmides, L., 1–18, 19, 21, 25–32, 36, 41–42, 54–58, 61, 74, 90–98, 115–120, 125, 138–140, 154, 156n9
Cummins, D., 12, 62, 121–122, 125

Damasio, A. R., 121
Darwinian
    algorithms (*see* Reasoning theories, Darwinian)
    modules (*see* Module, Darwinian; Justification, Darwinian module)
    semantics, 72–74
Davidson, D., 45, 157ch3n2
Dawes, R., 157n13
Dennett, D., 45, 88, 155n1
Deontic reasoning theories. *See* Reasoning theories, deontic and indicative